LET THE
BUNKER BURN

LET THE BUNKER BURN

The Final Battle With MOVE

CHARLES W. BOWSER

CAMINO BOOKS
Philadelphia

Manufactured in the United States of America

1 2 3 4 5 92 91 90 89

Library of Congress Cataloging-in-Publication Data

Bowser, Charles W.
  Let the bunker burn / by Charles W. Bowser

    p. cm.
    ISBN 0-940159-08-2
    1. MOVE (Organization) 2. Afro-Americans—Pennsylvania-
Philadelphia—Politics and government. 3. Black nationalism-
Pennsylvania—Philadelphia.4.Goode, W. Wilson.
    5. Philadelphia (Pa.) —Race relations. I. Title

    F158.9.N4B68 1989   CIP 89-505
    974.8'1100496073—dc 19

For information write:

Publisher
Camino Books
P.O. Box 59026
Philadelphia, PA. 19102

Cover Design: Amy Blake

CONTENTS

This book is dedicated to the members of the Philadelphia Special
Investigation Commission, which is known as the MOVE Commission:

William H. Brown, III Chairman
Rev. Audrey F. Bronson
Julia Chinn
M. Todd Cooke
Rev. Msgr. Edward P. Cullen
Justice Bruce W. Kauffman
Charisse R. Lillie, Esquire
Henry S. Ruth, Jr., Esquire
Rev. Paul M. Washington
Neil J. Welch, Esquire

PREFACE

History is replete with accounts of governmental atrocities more heinous than the tragedy this book is about. Genocide, torture, enslavement and other oppressions have been instruments of public policy employed by every form of government in every hemisphere. That women and innocent children were killed by the intentional acts of their local government is not new, but the context of the tragedy of May 13, 1985 is unique. Political, economic, social cultural or religious imperatives, based on bigotry justified by might, provided the rationalizations for historic atrocities.

The final battle with the MOVE cult, on Osage Avenue in Philadelphia, happened in an American city when the nation could justifiably claim an era of enlightenment. It was twenty years after racial discrimination had been destroyed as a legal entity. Black men were the mayors of three of the five largest cities in the country, including Philadelphia. The President of the Philadelphia City Council and the Superintendent of Philadelphia's public schools were black. The Chief Justice of the Pennsylvania Supreme Court was black. Black executives shared the suites of power in the city's corporate community, in academia and in civic organizations.

There was no reason to believe that the lives of black women and children would be held less dear than those of any other group. There was no reason to believe that the homes and property of the black residents of the Osage neighborhood would be callously and maliciously destroyed. There was no reason to believe that city police would fire high caliber automatic weapons into a row house where children trembled in fear. There was no reason to believe that city police would, at the direction of their superiors and with the approval of the mayor, make a bomb and drop it on the same house.

As unreasonable as it was, it happened. This book was written because it happened, and because it must not be forgotten. This book tells the story of what happened, who was responsible for what happened, who tried to prevent it, and who tried to hide it. This is also the story of how it happened. It is a story of inaction, mis-action and intended action which combined to create a tragedy of errors and malice.

Most atrocities produce only victims and villains, but this one produced a few heroes. They were unheard when they tried to prevent the events which defined the tragedy, and they were unheralded in its aftermath. None of the heroes were in positions of power and no one in power was heroic.

Five innocent children suffered terribly in the last moments of their lives. Their lungs were clogged with thick smoke and their bodies were wracked by the pain of burning flesh or hot bullets as they died. Their deaths made this version of what happened and how it happened necessary.

Why this atrocity happened depends on individual beliefs. Those who believe that our socio-political order has achieved enlightenment may conclude that it was an unfortunate accident resulting from gross negligence but completely unintentional. Those who despise all forms of order and authority may conclude that it was a diabolical drama of murder for some evil purpose. One conclusion is certain, the compassion of human governments cannot be taken for granted.

MOMENT OF DECISION

Five of Philadelphia's most powerful political leaders met in the home of Mayor W. Wilson Goode. They arrived before dawn on Monday, May 13, 1985. They came in response to the mayor's invitation and his warning, "I'm going to make a move on the MOVE house on Monday morning." Goode greeted each of the leaders and escorted them into the kitchen. They sipped coffee and awaited the police action scheduled to begin at 6 A.M. The kitchen was at the rear of the upper level of the split level house. The kitchen's rear door opened onto a small balcony overlooking the rear yard. It was a thick lawn, the size of a little league football field. Goode lived about 23 blocks from the MOVE house at 6221 Osage Avenue.

Joseph Coleman, President of the City Council; Lucien Blackwell, Chairman of the Finance Committee of City Council; State Senator Hardy Williams, and the mayor had known each other since the early 1960's. They helped to spawn the demand for black political power that disrupted the political status quo in Philadelphia. State Representative Peter Truman was closest to the neighborhood problems which brought them together. The MOVE family lived within Districts represented by Blackwell, Williams and Truman. They knew there had to be a response to the disorder, anger and fear which consumed the Osage Avenue neighborhood. Each of them had previous experiences with MOVE. They were convinced some action had to be taken. But they had no involvement in planning the police operation.

Truman's office had been besieged by complaining constituents. They demanded immediate relief from myriad grievances against MOVE. He wanted the problem solved, but he understood the hazards of a confrontation. Three days earlier he told the mayor, "You know there is going to be gunfire, and MOVE has made threats to blow up the entire neighborhood if they are attacked." Truman's district hummed with whispered reports of tunnels, dug by MOVE beneath Osage Avenue, and of gallons of gasoline stored by MOVE members on the roofs of their neighbors' houses.

Truman was impressed by the potential for a disaster, and he was concerned for the safety of the children who lived in the MOVE house. It was after 7 P.M. when he left the mayor's office on May 10. The mayor assured him every precaution would be taken to protect the children. He was told the police would not shoot into the house to return gunfire if that would endanger the children. The mayor had given similar assurances to each of the leaders. Therefore they did not discuss the operation as they sat in the small kitchen awaiting reports from Osage Avenue. The kitchen was equipped as a communications center. There was a small television, a police radio and a telephone with a direct line to the command post at the scene.

The mayor told them City Managing Director Leo Brooks, a retired Army general, was supervising the operation at the scene and he would report to them. The first reports they heard were the sounds of automatic weapons. They were tense. They had not anticipated the ominous reports of heavy caliber weapons. They did not know who was receiving the fire. If heavy caliber automatic weapons were fired at police that was bad. If they were fired into the house, where children might be hurt, that was worse.

The mayor relayed messages from Brooks that the automatic weapons were fired by MOVE members but no one was injured. According to the mayor, Brooks reported, "MOVE has opened fire on the police with .50-caliber machine guns in all directions." They stepped from the kitchen onto the rear balcony to hear better the sounds of the battle.

Coleman said, "Well that certainly justifies the use of force. If they are using .50-caliber machine guns that justifies the use of police force."

Despite the report of heavy weapons fire from the MOVE house, the mayor relayed a report from Brooks that police were following the plan to shoot above the house to protect the children. The mayor relayed a report of a white male running through the area, shooting at police. Brooks thought he might have been a

MOVE sympathizer. There was a report that a police officer was wounded and taken to the hospital.

They huddled close to the mayor as he tried to determine the extent of the officer's wounds. They did not want their leadership tarnished by the death of a police officer. The 1978 confrontation between the police and MOVE resulted in the death of Officer James Ramp. They expected a better result. They expected a safe and peaceful confrontation. They expected too much.

The mayor's communication channels did not provide the information about the injured officer. It was a significant failure. It was an early symptom of fatal flaws in the operation; a harbinger of the disaster. Police guards, stationed outside the mayor's house, told them the officer was not wounded. He was taken to the hospital because he was overcome by fatigue. Coleman sat at the kitchen table engrossed in television reports of the battle. After watching tons of water and clouds of tear gas directed at the house, he told the mayor those tactics were excessive. The shooting stopped. The water and tear gas failed to force a surrender. Williams knew the police plan would not succeed. He said to the mayor, "Why don't they just back up and relax? No one is going anywhere."

It was good and timely advice. Williams had been Goode's political ally and personal friend. They were among the founders of the Black Political Forum. In 1971, Goode was manager of Williams' campaign for mayor. They had made political plans in hundreds of meetings as they persisted in demanding increased black participation in elected and appointed offices.

They were no longer rebellious outsiders as they sat in Goode's kitchen. History had rewarded them with the moment they fought for: the moment of decision. Five hundred police officers were engaged in a black neighborhood, and they were in charge. They were where they imagined their white predecessors had been, sitting in a room, determining the fate of black people. It was the first time in the city's history that black leaders had the power to cancel a police operation. Their concern for the problems confronting them obscured their historic precedent. Because they were not focused on the racial dimensions of their leadership, the moment was lost. Also lost was the opportunity to avoid a tragedy.

Black political leaders across the country had come to positions of responsibility too complex to be understood and defined in purely racial terms. Their blackness was not enough to help them precisely discern the merits and pitfalls of their options. The mayor invited them to his home because of their official capacities, not because of their common political history.

The weight of official responsibility relegated them to their official roles. Goode invited them to share the responsibility of the moment, but that was not possible. They could advise him, but he must decide.

The dramatic events of that morning were an exaggeration of problems in other localities where black leaders who had been outside of government, demanding change, found themselves saddled with the responsibility to make change. What they decided, in each instance, was not as important as how they defined their responsibilities. No matter what the outcome of their decisions, the status quo remained intact if they could not match their responsibilities to their commitments. Their options were not unlike those available to their white predecessors. Their choices were not easy. Most of them required decisions which would hurt someone. As political rebels, Goode and his allies were comrades. They were committed to a single cause. Their camaraderie overcame disputes and disagreements. Their common foes were the mortar of their unity. As elected officials they learned about the division of power between the executive and legislative branches of government. They learned about the shifting tolerances of influence involved in the checks and balances of the governmental structure. They learned about the safety of not assuming the problems of another branch of government.

They were willing to make suggestions. They were willing to offer their support, but they could not accept or assume the responsibility. That belonged to the executive branch of government—the mayor.

That is why leadership is lonely in America. Presidents, governors and mayors testify to the loneliness. When the crunch comes, the community, the state or the nation places upon them the burden of decision. That loneliness, which forces a leader to examine his values and his motives in an effort to reach the right decision, is one of the most human qualities of democratic government. It is the human test of the ability of a democratic society to develop, and elevate to leadership, persons who personify the moral fortitude, personal values and intellectual honesty the society cherishes.

In those moments of decision leaders are dependent on the information and opinions supplied by their subordinates. Effective leaders do not need expertise in the disciplines of the people they lead, but they must have the skill to orchestrate and validate those disciplines. President Lyndon Johnson relied on information and opinions from military leaders about Vietnam. He did not effectively question them and test their information or their opinions. The painful result was the destruction of his presidency.

Goode had every reason to heed Williams' advice. Before the leaders left, he knew the report that MOVE members had fired .50-caliber machine guns was not true. He knew the police were not shooting above the house. He knew the children in the house were in danger. He knew the police plan was not working.

He did not respond to Williams. The other leaders asked him how he thought the operation would develop. They wanted to know if they should cancel their appointments and remain with him. The mayor assured them the police would continue to use water and tear gas to force the MOVE members out of the house. He said, "Time is on our side."

Goode was alone when the leaders left to attend to their duties. From the balcony beyond the kitchen's rear door, he could look down on the bright spring greenness of his rear yard. He could hear the reports of weapons fired on Osage Avenue. The other leaders had been sympathetic and supportive, but he realized they could not share the burdens of that day.

He was adrift on a sea of troubles which could become a tidal wave of disaster. He had selected and appointed the city officials who were directing the battle. He established the policy which authorized the plan for the police operation. He had not questioned and tested the information and opinions of his field commanders. He had not probed to make them justify the critical aspects of their plan.

Spring freshness was in the air when he left his home for his office in City Hall. By nightfall the stench of smoke arising from burning buildings on Osage Avenue filled the air for miles. Before dawn his leadership was criticized in every major city of the nation. Osage Avenue became one of the best known streets in the world. The mayor and the street forged a tragic place in human history. When he left his home for City Hall the elements of his failures were moving inexorably toward the disaster which would scar his record as mayor. Flames, black smoke, charred rubble and the broken bodies of children would permanently shadow his career. Public scrutiny of his failures on that day and debate of his competence would challenge his confidence and his self-esteem.

His failure would test the political loyalty of Philadelphia's black voters and diminish his standing as a national leader. In 1983, he was swept into office on a tidal wave of black pride and a greater percentage of white votes than any previous black candidate received. He was the heroic symbol of Philadelphia's political progress. In 1984 he was interviewed as a potential vice-presidential running mate by Walter Mondale, the Democratic candidate for president. Until May 13, 1985, the city had been proud of its mayor. Until that day he managed the reins of power well. He had been decisive, effective and respected.

Before daylight left the sky, he would become the first American mayor to author a disaster of presidential proportions. Ordinarily the failures of mayors have no impact beyond their local communities. Presidents of the United States perform in an international theater where their successes and failures regularly generate global responses.

The global response to the Osage Avenue tragedy elevated the mayor's failure to a par with President Kennedy's failure in the Bay of Pigs invasion of Cuba, President Lyndon Johnson's failures in the Vietnam war, President Jimmy Carter's failed rescue of hostages held by Iran, and President Ronald Reagan's failures which cost the lives of 249 Marines in Beirut, and 31 seamen in the Persian Gulf. The scope and complexity of national and international conflicts may justify the risks which presidents sometimes take. The potential advancement of national interests sometimes balances the extent of the disasters which accompany failure.

The city's conflict with the residents of the house at 6221 Osage Avenue, and the problems involved in serving four of them with arrest warrants, should not have created a disaster of international proportions. Unlike presidents who have failed on foreign soil against a foreign adversary, the mayor failed on a city street where almost any American could have lived—where most Americans believe they should be protected from unrestrained violence.

That basic protection was at the center of a mayor's duty. His mission involved more than the administration of city services. Inherent in the democratic process is the obligation of elected leaders to protect and enhance personal liberty. When, as a result of their failure, life, liberty and property are destroyed, the tragedy transcends the material losses. It extends to a loss of confidence in traditions, a loss of security in the present and a loss of faith in the future.

On May 14, dawn's gray light illuminated the wreckage of Mayor Goode's worst day in office. The losses of life and property were apparent, but the broader losses of liberty were only emerging.

2

THE BOMB

Bill Klein ran toward the helicopter. He carried a green tear gas canister bag and a white canvas bag. His commander, Police Lt. Frank Powell, was seated behind the helicopter pilots. He was putting on a harness which allowed him to lean out the helicopter door. Klein handed both bags to Powell. He shouted, above the roar of the helicopter engine, "Use the gas bag first." The helicopter engine roared louder as the copter prepared to lift off. Klein shouted his instructions again, "Use the gas bag first."

The helicopter took off from 63rd and Walnut Streets in West Philadelphia shortly after 5:20 P.M. It circled and approached 6221 Osage Avenue from a northerly direction. Once they were airborne, Powell radioed firefighters on the ground. His target was the bunker on the roof of 6221 Osage. He ordered the firefighters to train their water cannons on the bunker. The deluge was intended to force down and neutralize any snipers in the bunker. As the helicopter passed over the roof, the water cannons were turned off to afford Powell a clear view of the target. The pilot positioned the helicopter for the steep approach to the target they had rehearsed. Their plan was to dive in quickly, then hover above the roof. Powell would lean out of the copter's door and drop a bag of explosives. On Powell's command the pilot would take off in a 90-degree turn to the right. The pilot dove toward the roof. Before he could bring the helicopter to an absolute hover, he saw Powell toss out the bag. The pilot immediately pulled away without waiting for Powell's command. They flew about half a mile due west where they waited for the explosion intended to end the violent confrontation between the City of Philadelphia and MOVE.

Powell, Klein and the other members of the police Bomb
Disposal Unit had been on duty since 10 P.M. the night before when
they packed explosives, weapons and other gear for the operation
against the MOVE house. As the day wore on, it became clear that
the police could not accomplish their mission so long as the
bunker gave the high ground advantage to the MOVE combatants.
It was the police commissioner's job to solve the problem of the
bunker.

By the time the helicopter took off, Police Commissioner
Gregore Sambor and most of his men had been on duty for more
than fifteen hours. Some of his men visited the residents of the
6200 block of Osage Avenue on Sunday night to evacuate them
before the operation began. Most of the residents were happy to
cooperate, because for more than a year they had been awaiting
action by the city to solve the neighborhood problem which made
their lives unbearable.

The police instructed them to take enough of their
possessions for Sunday night and Monday, and assured them they
would be able to return to their homes Monday night. By Monday
night the police operation would have ended, and the residents of
6221 Osage Avenue would have been removed from that house.
Their powerful loudspeakers, through which they assaulted their
neighbors with abusive profanity, would have been dismantled.
The torment of terror and frustration would end.

That was the assurance the evacuees received, because that
was the plan. The evacuees dispersed to the homes of family and
friends to await the signal to return. By 4:30 in the afternoon many
of them had returned, without being summoned. Drawn to the
scene by television reports of the progress of the operation, they
gathered with hundreds of other residents from the immediate
neighborhood to watch from behind police barriers.

They saw a gun battle on their street, they saw giant cranes
hoisting hoses to spray tons of water onto the rooftop bunker
at 6221 Osage, and they heard intermittent explosions on their
street. The confidence they felt when they left their homes was
fading. The city's solution of the problem was beginning to cause
them as much concern as the problem itself. Something was
wrong; it was taking too long to remove the people from 6221.

Many of the other spectators at the barricades understood
the torment suffered by the evacuees, but they began to grumble
about the amount of force the police were using on the small row
house. They expressed their deep concern for the safety of the

children who lived in 6221 Osage, and they wondered why the battle had to be fought in their neighborhood.

Unrest, uneasiness and fatigue charged the environment as the neighborhood and the entire city watched the police assault bog down and then stop. Despite superior numbers and weapons, the police were stymied by the tactical advantage of the bunker.

It was built as a combat bunker should be built. The force of the water cannons did not budge it, and police weapons could not pierce it. Whoever manned the bunker had the advantage. Its gun ports commanded the front and rear of the MOVE house. By 4:30 in the afternoon, Sambor knew the bunker had to go, or the evacuees would not return to their homes that day. He knew the bunker had to go, or he would have to keep his men on duty through the night, because he had not made plans to relieve them. He knew the bunker had to go, because there were rumors that the MOVE people dug tunnels under the street. He thought they might place explosives under the buildings where his men were stationed. He knew the bunker had to go, because television cameras were recording how a few combatants in a single house were thwarting the Philadelphia Police Department.

Police fired more than ten thousand bullets into the house. Explosive charges were thrown into the house. But nightfall was coming, and the police were no closer to evicting the occupants of 6221 Osage than they had been at dawn.

Local television stations pre-empted their normal schedule of programs to focus the attention of the city on the West Philadelphia battleground. National television networks joined in the broad-casts, relaying the details and significance of the neighborhood problem to the nation and the world.

The nation was watching the Philadelphia Police Department at work. Not since the Vietnam war was broadcast live into American homes, had a battle scene attracted so much interest. The drama was heightened by the prospect that John Africa, the founder and prophet of the cult, might be in the house.

The unrest and uneasiness spread beyond the ranks of the spectators at the police barricades. People who had not heard about MOVE wanted to know more about it. But most of all, everyone wanted to know why it was taking so long for the police to overpower one house.

At 3 P.M. Mayor Goode summoned the press into the ornate chamber which served as the mayor's reception room. It was one of the jewels of the late Victorian architecture of City Hall. The huge doors to the room were hung on thick brass hinges decorated with etchings. Portraits of former mayors hung on the walls just beneath cornices of carved wood.

It was the room where mayors of the city officially welcomed heads of state and other dignitaries. It was a grand and dignified room. Usually its ambiance made visitors lower their voices and modify their behavior.

The news reporters summoned by Mayor Goode were unimpressed. They pursued the developing story with the ferocity of piranhas at mealtime. They shouted at him; they cross-examined him; they badgered him, and they drew from him the ominous declaration that it was the city's intention to remove the MOVE members from the house "by any means necessary."

At 3 P.M. on May 13, it was a provocative declaration. Weeks later, when it was replayed during the hearings of the commission investigating the tragedy that concluded the operation, it was a chilling declaration of total war. But none of the reporters who heard and recorded the mayor's declaration understood the full context surrounding that declaration. They did not know that "any means necessary" would include a bomb dropped from a helicopter on to the roof of a row house in which there were at least six children.

Some of the reporters probed for a definition of the intensity and extent of the conflict. "Are negotiations still possible?" one asked.

Earlier Mayor Goode told them the city's efforts at negotiation had failed, and he made the decision to enforce warrants for the arrest of four of the residents of the house. Later a small group of community leaders requested an opportunity to try to persuade the MOVE members to surrender. "It is my feeling that we should try to negotiate until we determine that we cannot negotiate any longer," Mayor Goode replied. In response to questions about the negotiators, he explained they were "a group of clergymen and heads of organizations and members of varied groups around the city who have been active in things like this across the years. I don't know their names, I did not take their names."

He sent them to speak with City Managing Director Leo Brooks. Brooks was the ranking city official at the scene; the mayor instructed him to permit the volunteer negotiators to try to resolve the conflict peacefully.

The negotiators were good people with good intentions, but they had no authority to offer anything to the MOVE members.

Their faith was in the values they lived by. They believed that adults always protected children and preserved life. They did not understand the magnitude of the challenge the MOVE members were making to the system. Their pleas for reasonable compromise were as unheeded as a sigh in a hurricane.

In war even the lives of children are forfeit to the exigencies of ideology and power. The MOVE members in 6221 Osage Avenue had declared war against their neighbors. It began as psychological warfare. Christmas Eve, 1983, marked the first profane diatribe which blared from MOVE loudspeakers.

Night after night, the Osage neighbors heard themselves vilified by name. They could not shield their children; they could not protect their personal dignity. They were called "motherfuckers," "whores," "bitches" and worse. The language was not new to the adults, but it was a new experience for their children. Before Christmas Eve, 1983, the children had lived in a reasonably safe, sane and satisfying world. They attended school, played games on the street where they lived and watched the television shows their parents permitted.

Most of their parents moved to Osage Avenue from less desirable neighborhoods. They wanted their children to advance farther than they had. They wanted their children to see a better, brighter slice of life than they saw. They wanted them to live in a nourishing environment and to develop into good citizens. They wanted no more than the common dream of every not-so-common American family; but because they were black families, they wanted it longer and more fervently. They were innocent victims of a MOVE strategy to force legal authorities to release cult members who had been imprisoned for murder. MOVE members were convinced the system would free their imprisoned compatriots in exchange for an end to the psychological hostilities.

So it was that the mayor faced a crowded room of reporters, the volunteer negotiators faced a fortified house and pleaded for peace, the police faced the frustration of their inability to assert legal authority, and Police Commissioner Sambor faced an end to rational options for victory.

John Africa and his followers clenched their weapons in the shadows of the fortified house. Their defiance was not softened by entreaties from negotiators. They had engineered the final test of their own convictions, and they knew only one conclusion was possible. As the mayor talked with reporters about negotiations, and about his hope for a peaceful conclusion, he, too, knew only one conclusion was possible.

The reality of violence as a solution to any problem is that it eliminates moral, ethical and intellectual distinctions between the adversaries. Each side is reduced to a common denominator of aggression which obfuscates the problem with a torrent of pain and destruction.

Only the courageous negotiators believed the final, fatal torrent of violence could be prevented. They did not know Sambor had a deadline for completing the operation, or at least the mayor told the reporters he had a deadline. When he was asked how long he would allow the standoff to continue, the mayor said that the operational decisions would be made by Sambor. When he was asked if Sambor had established a deadline, he replied, "None which I will discuss with you."

The limit of the city's restraint was breached when the profane harangue continued beyond one year. Another less discernible limit would be crossed before nightfall. As the tension of the crisis increased, fatigue eroded the delicate balance of emotion and intellect which allows for rationality.

The mayor's attention had been focused the entire day on that single block of the city. There must have been some erosion of sensitivity and flexibility which influenced the momentous decision he would make about two hours after the press conference ended.

There was a moment, confused by conflicting recollections of its content and obscured by the events that followed it, when power, public posture, ideology, frustration and malice were submerged, and delaying the operation until the following day was considered. Delay would have violated the deadline, but it also could have eliminated the bomb as an option for concluding the operation.

Five months later, when Mayor Goode, General Brooks and Commissioner Sambor were questioned by the commission investigating the tragedy, the deadline to which the mayor alluded during the press conference had disappeared. Sambor told the commission, "I was not in any hurry. I was . . . I did not feel under any obligation whatsoever to complete the mission that day."

Sambor also said that he did not discuss completing the operation by nightfall. He admitted there were problems with continuing the operation after dark, but he was certain he did not discuss those problems in detail with Brooks.

When Mayor Goode was asked by the commission if a dead-line was set for completing the operation he answered, "There was none that I'm aware of that was expressed. And to my knowledge, there was not any reason that we had to go that day."

In response to the query as to why they did not opt to wait until the next day to regroup and reconsider their position, Sambor said, "Because we had several hours of daylight and if putting the hole in the roof and eliminating the bunker could have been effected that evening, it would have presented us and put us in a better situation for the next day or even that evening."

Brooks told the commission a different story. Contrary to Sambor's claim that delay was not discussed in any detail, Brooks said it was discussed at great length. He said, "And the conclusions were that we had a very difficult situation because we knew there was a labyrinth; we thought there was a labyrinth of tunnels . . . and if that was the case, that there were probably some escape routes. Secondly, we knew that it was very difficult to secure that area. The alley there is very narrow behind those houses. There was no place to set up the typical kind of searchlight light business that the Police Department normally does with great care. You would have had to change the people. And there were many other things of that nature that made it difficult. Plus neighbors were already in the street agitating to get back into their homes and the agitation was on 63rd Street as well as over on 62nd Street and back around in Pine where we had them pushed across the intersection. And we had people out there from Human Relations and what-not helping to calm, trying to get the residents to go back to the church and other places to be quiet. So there were many things . . . that helped to influence or cause an effort to continue and resolve it that day."

The Brooks version is consistent with what could be reason-ably expected during an event of that magnitude within a residen-tial neighborhood. The opportunity to delay, regroup and reconsider was lost because there was a deadline—deadline created by the pressures of the moment and a deadline implicit in the city government's determination to be done with MOVE, once and for all.

A history of hostility, violence and defiance of legal authority was part of the context that developed on Osage Avenue as the shadows of the houses began to extend farther and farther eastward toward 62nd Street and the battle was stalemated. The Federal Bureau of Investigation, the Alcohol, Tobacco and Firearms division of the United States Treasury Department, the Pennsylvania State Police, as well as the state and federal courts had been involved in the evolution of the MOVE cult from an obscure group of extreme naturalists to an openly profane and provocative challenger of all legal authority.

The determination to be rid of MOVE was not verbalized but it was evident. Sambor alluded to a part of the police department's previous relationship with MOVE in his opening statement to the investigating commission. He said, "In preparing for the confrontation that they consciously chose, we had lessons from sad experience. In the spring of 1977, we had hoped that armed threats would disappear if pacified. By the fall of that year, we had thought that an indefinite state of siege—a siege almost one year as it turned out—would starve MOVE into submission. By August of 1978, we hoped that an overpowering police presence—a frontal attack—would intimidate MOVE to peaceful surrender."

As it turned out the experience of previous attempts to subdue MOVE did not teach the police much about tactics and strategy when confronted by a dedicated intransigent adversary, but it must have fueled the determination to be done with MOVE.

There was also the memory of Police Officer James Ramp who was killed during the 1978 confrontation with other MOVE members at another location. Sambor was determined not to suffer the death or wounding of any police officers. It is therefore not coincidental that at 3:30 P.M., half an hour after he learned that Police Sgt. Edward Connor of the bomb squad had been knocked to the ground by a .38-caliber bullet, Sambor told Powell to prepare for the possibility of using explosives on the roof.

Sgt. Connor was not wounded by the bullet, which struck the back of his bullet-proof vest. The incident was reported on the police radio. Police in firing positions were tense as they remembered the death of Officer Ramp.

Between 4 P.M. and 5 P.M. Sambor pushed inexorably toward the bomb. He asked the volunteer negotiators to make one last attempt to persuade the MOVE members to surrender, but he did not tell them about the alternative to surrender he had under active consideration. The mother of Theresa Brooks Africa used a police bullhorn to try to convince her daughter to come out of the house and to bring the children.

It was the day after Mothers' Day, but a bullhorn does not enhance the parental quality of the human voice. Amplification exaggerates vocal flaws and overwhelms emotional qualities. A mother speaking through a bullhorn sounds no less officious than a police commander. If Theresa was alive at 4:20 when her mother called to her, she was wet and cold from the tons of water cannonaded onto the house. She was probably hungry, because combat had not provided a respite for a meal, and she was probably afraid.

If her mother could have reached her she would have done it before Theresa joined MOVE. If her mother could have reached her she would not have been crouching in the darkened rooms of a house under attack by the police. John Africa had reached her. He had invaded her mind and occupied it to the exclusion of her mother and every other contrary voice. Theresa did not respond to her mother. When Theresa added "Africa" to her name, she embraced MOVE for life. None of the MOVE members responded to any of the final entreaties to surrender.

While the negotiators pleaded for surrender, Sambor, Brooks and Fire Commissioner William Richmond were meeting to discuss the options left to them. They received a report that a plan to use a construction crane to lift the bunker from the roof was not feasible because the crane operator might be shot.

By 4 P.M. they agreed to Sambor's plan to use explosives, and they summoned Powell and Klein to meet them in the basement of the Walnut Park Plaza Apartments and Geriatric Center at 63rd and Walnut Streets, across 63rd Street from the helicopter pad.

In its heyday the apartment building was a preferred address near the western boundary of the city. Its architecture reflected a pretense of elegance that partially mimicked mid-Victorian architectural attempts at splendor. In the late fifties, after the Korean war, the neighborhood welcomed the first middle class black families to live west of an economic and ethnic border at 60th Street. After that, fear, racial prejudice and the chance to sell old houses at exorbitant prices resulted in an ethnic conversion of the neighborhood around Walnut Plaza.

The apartment building suffered from the combination of withdrawal of investment capital, bank red-lining and depressed rents. Eventually the building was converted to senior citizen apartments and a geriatric center. It was also the command post for the combined forces of the city, stationed three blocks away surrounding the 6200 block of Osage Avenue.

Powell was 41 years old and a 17-year veteran of the Philadelphia Police Department. He began his career as a beat policeman and after two and a half years earned a promotion to detective. Three years later he became a sergeant, and two and a half years later he was promoted to lieutenant. As a lieutenant he was assigned to the Juvenile Aid Division, and he was chief of the Morals and Sex Offenses Squad before he was assigned to the Stakeout Bomb Unit in January 1979.

Later Stakeout became a separate unit, and in 1984 Powell was made commanding officer of the Bomb Disposal Unit attached to the Philadelphia Police Academy. During his 17 years as a policeman he had 45 days of training in explosive disposal and related areas. Thirty of the 45 days was training he received after May 13, 1985.

Officer Klein, who accompanied Powell to the meeting with the commanders, was 38 years old, and a 13 year veteran of the police force. His training with explosives began in the United States Marine Corps between 1964 and 1968. He earned the rank of gunnery sergeant specializing in explosive ordinance disposal. He completed the course in demolition and land mine warfare at Camp LeJeune, North Carolina.

While serving in Vietnam he used explosives to open enemy tunnels, to destroy fortifications, to remove booby traps and to destroy caches of weapons. In Vietnam he preferred to use the military explosive designated "C-4" because it was pliable like putty, not likely to explode without planned detonation and very powerful. As a policeman he was trained in explosives by the Bureau of Alcohol, Tobacco and Firearms and the Federal Bureau of Investigation.

It was a combat meeting on the field of battle. Sambor, Powell and Klein were dressed in black paratrooper jump suits and wore black baseball-type caps. Klein was armed with a .357mm magnum revolver, a 9mm city-issued Model 39 automatic pistol with two extra magazines, a mini-Uzzi submachine gun with four magazines, a Marine Corps K-Bar knife, a half-mile light, a flashlight, a gas mask and two canteens of water.

Earlier, when Sambor told Powell to prepare for the possibility of using an explosive charge to eliminate the bunker, Powell sent a member of the bomb squad to the explosive storage magazine at the Police Academy to obtain a supply of Tovex TR2. Tovex TR2 was a commercial explosive developed as an alternative to dynamite in the 1960's. It was designed to dig trenches through rock to lay pipes. The "TR" stands for trench and the "2" stands for the second DuPont product in the trenching line.

DuPont's Explosive Products Division was located in

Wilmington, Delaware, about forty miles from Philadelphia. No one from the Philadelphia Police Department contacted DuPont on or before May 13, when Powell decided Tovex was the explosive of choice to be dropped on a residential neighborhood. If an inquiry had been made, Philadelphia authorities would have learned that Tovex TR2 had been used exclusively underground, and DuPont scientists had no idea what might happen if it were used above ground.

Brooks believed he was meeting with police explosives experts. Sambor told him Powell was an expert with great training and a significant amount of experience. Therefore Brooks asked one question about the explosives they planned to drop on 6221 Osage. He asked how much the explosive would weigh. Powell said it would weigh two pounds and Sambor repeated his answer to Brooks.

Two pounds of what? Three months later, when Powell recalled the meeting about the bomb, he was certain none of his superiors asked him which explosive he would use. His recollection was that they were only concerned with blowing the bunker off the roof, and, as a secondary objective, making a hole in the roof. Klein also recalled that there was no mention of the explosive to be employed, and he further recalled there was no discussion of fire or safety considerations.

Klein recalled that Brooks asked if the bomb could be made and dropped quietly, and Sambor asked if it could be done before nightfall. Sambor's later recollection was that Tovex was discussed as the explosive to be used and also that there was discussion of tests of Tovex on materials similar to the roof of 6221 Osage.

None of them knew what they were talking about. Brooks, Sambor and Richmond relied entirely on the expertise of Powell and Klein. Neither Powell nor Klein had ever constructed an explosive device which was intended to perform a specific task after being dropped from a helicopter. Whatever their training had been, they were not trained in making and dropping bombs.

As soon as Powell and Klein left the meeting, Powell told Klein to return to the bomb disposal truck and make an explosive device of two sticks of Tovex TR2, two inches by sixteen inches, and place it in a satchel with a fuse. Klein didn't think Powell knew as much about explosives as he did, and he decided to mix some C-4 with the Tovex to move the bunker and cut a hole in the roof. Klein decided to exercise his independent judgment and overrule his superiors. He claimed he placed a 1¼-pound block of C-4 on top of two sticks of Tovex that weighed about a pound each.

A scientific study of pictures of the blast created by Klein's bomb, compared to test blasts of various combinations of Tovex and C-4, demonstrated that Klein's bomb had the characteristics of an explosion by a device containing three 1¼-pound blocks of C-4 and two sticks of Tovex.

Powell and Klein told investigators that their unit had only about one pound of C-4 which was used to train dogs to detect explosives. Local police departments obtained C-4 from the military or from federal law enforcement agencies. In 1979 the United States Army ended distribution of C-4 to local police departments.

On August 19, 1985, the assistant director of the Philadelphia office of the FBI wrote to investigators that small remnant amounts of C-4 explosive had been periodically furnished to the Philadelphia police for training purposes. That letter was a cover-up that was corrected by the special agent in charge of the Philadelphia FBI office. In a letter dated October 22, 1985, he admitted that in January approximately thirty blocks of C-4 had been delivered to Philadelphia police by an FBI agent without their request. The FBI agent had prescribed to the police an extremely powerful military explosive at the very time that their major problem was an anticipated confrontation with MOVE. Each block of C-4 weighed 1¼ pounds.

About 5 P.M., as Klein was in the bomb disposal truck making the bombs and Powell was in the helicopter practicing their dropping, Brooks telephoned Mayor Goode. It was his second call to the mayor in fifteen minutes. During the first call he told the mayor that the possibility of placing explosives on the roof was under consideration.

After Powell and Klein left the Walnut Plaza meeting, Brooks turned in his chair and picked up the telephone. He dialed the mayor and told him, "The Commissioner has come to the conclusion that if we have to resolve this before dark he's got to get tear gas in; the only way we know how to do it is to enter the roof with some device that might also blow the bunker off when it happens and it will be delivered from the helicopter."

Brooks also told the mayor, "It's going to be difficult to secure the area during the night. The neighbors are clamoring to return to their homes; it would be difficult to light the dark alleys."

Mayor Goode listened, and then thought about it for thirty seconds before he asked, "Does Mr. Sambor know about this?"

Brooks replied, "Yes, it was his idea."

The mayor then asked Brooks if he believed it would work, and Brooks said they all believed it would work. The mayor next asked when the explosives would be used, and Brooks told him in about twenty minutes.

Then the mayor said, "Okay. Keep me posted."

The bomb was approved by the highest city authority; there was nothing left to stop it.

Detective William Stephenson was at his post along the tree line of Cobbs Creek Drive and Osage Avenue. He had been there most of the day taking notes on the operation. According to his notes at 5:25 P.M., water deluge guns started spraying the MOVE house. Three minutes later the State Police helicopter, with Powell on board, made two passes over the house. Stephenson had a clear view of the bag of explosives dropped from the helicopter.

About a minute later, 5:29 P.M., there was a loud explosion on the roof, followed immediately by a large, bright orange ball of flame. Debris flew from the roof above the front bunker in a southerly direction. The bunker shook briefly, but it was not moved. Stephenson saw a small amount of black and white smoke and a small flame on the roof.

By 5:51 P.M., Stephenson reported, "massive amounts of black smoke and a small flame is coming from 6221 Osage." Eight minutes later the fire spread to the front of the house with ten-foot-high dark orange flames. A slight breeze arose and blew the fire westward.

Twenty minutes later there were twenty-foot-high flames and black smoke coming out of the second floor window of the house. Within five minutes the flames were fifty feet high and the house next door, 6219 Osage, was on fire.

At 6:30 P.M. the fire department made its first attempt to put water on the fire. It was too late.

3

LET THE BUNKER BURN

> It was a judgment decision . . . I will have to live with. I have a set
> of regrets on one point, and that is the four children which I have
> grieved very, very greatly for. But on the other hand, I don't have the
> other set of regrets to face and that is the death of a police or
> firefighter, ...
>
> *Fire Commissioner William Richmond*

The fire was started when the bomb blast generated 7200 degrees
Fahrenheit, splintered heavy lumber into kindling and hurled it
across the roof into flames from a can of gasoline which was ignited
by the explosion. The process occurred during the millisecond of
the bomb's blast. General Brooks and Commissioner Sambor
watched from a ninth floor balcony of the Walnut Plaza. Brooks
focused his binoculars on the roof as the helicopter circled for its
final approach. The roof was littered with heavy timbers, and there
were cans marked "gasoline." Fire experts define wooden timbers
and similar items as "Class A" materials because they burn very
easily. They consider gasoline to be the same as dynamite.

An hour earlier, when Brooks, Sambor and Fire Commissioner Richmond were making the decision to drop the bomb on the
roof, no one suggested that they use the binoculars to inspect the
roof. The C-4 military explosive, which Klein added to the bomb,
greatly enhanced the blast and the heat of the explosion, and
increased the pyrolysis of the Class A material. The fire was

inevitable, even if the Class A material had not been present, because the roof was covered with tar. Tar is a petroleum distillate, and 7200 degrees Fahrenheit is enough to ignite it.

As soon as the flash of the explosion faded, Brooks saw a thin column of white smoke rise from the roof. Lt. Powell reported from the helicopter that there was no smoke and no fire. Eight to ten minutes later Brooks saw flames on the roof. White smoke was evidence that Class A materials had been ignited and an incipient fire had begun. At that point, the fire could have been extinguished by a fire extinguisher, a bucket of water, or by the squirts which had played torrents of water on the roof all day.

Sambor left the balcony after the explosion and did not see the flames that Brooks had reported on the police radio. Fire Commissioner Richmond was at 62nd and Osage when the bomb exploded. Eight to ten minutes after the explosion his aide said to him, "Chief, I think we have a fire on the roof." Richmond walked quickly to a nearby van in which a local television station had a monitor linked to a camera focused on the roof from a boom. The television picture verified his aide's claim. There was an incipient fire on the roof. It was about 5:37 P.M., and there was fire, wood, gasoline and tar on the roof. Richmond testified that he did not know there was gasoline on the roof. If he knew about the gasoline, his decisions on the bomb and the incipient fire would have been different. He said, "When you mention gas to a firefighter, you are talking dynamite. We had a lot of experience with this, day in and day out. And, yes, it would have ran a red flag right up."

As Sambor watched the fire developing, he thought there was some gasoline in the house. He knew the MOVE people had a gasoline-powered generator. He claimed that he did not know there was gasoline on the roof.

At least nine of his subordinates had confirmed the presence of cans marked "gasoline" on the roof prior to May 13. As early as May 2, Captain Edward McLaughlin, Commander of the Major Investigation Division, saw containers marked "gasoline" in aerial photographs of the MOVE house. The same information was shared by Lt. Powell, Sgt. Albert Revel, Officer Michael Tursi, Captain James Shanahan, Chief Inspector John Craig, Detectives Benner and Boyd and Inspector John Tiers. Sambor's ignorance of the information about the gasoline is peculiar, if not perfidious. The Major Investigations Division was created under Sambor's administration of the police department, and it reported directly to him. If it is true that McLaughlin did not report critical information to Sambor before May 13, then there was an incredible failure in communication. It is more likely that Sambor did receive the information, but he only considered it insofar as it may have endangered police personnel.

Brooks absolved himself of any knowledge of the gasoline when he said, "There were rumors of all sorts about what they would do. So one could in an unqualified sense say that that was information, because the information came from all kinds of sources. But to have what would appear to a reasonable person to be evidence that there is gasoline on the roof, I didn't have any such I didn't have that kind of information."

What about the official information that was available to him and to Sambor—information which they should have known and understood if they planned to use force to arrest four people? The search warrants and arrest warrants, which provided the legal provocation for the police operation, were based on sworn affidavits of a police officer. Among other things the officer swore that the MOVE members possessed "explosives and/or incendiary devices or material . . . ." Neither Brooks nor Sambor could recall reading the affidavits. They did not inform themselves about the allegations against the MOVE members. They didn't know if the allegations were serious enough to warrant the amount of force involved in ten thousand bullets, tear gas, tons of water, explosives and fire.

Mayor Goode knew about the gasoline on the roof before May 13. He did not tell the fire commissioner about the gasoline because he did not speak directly to the fire commissioner, and because he assumed everyone knew what he knew. When he took thirty seconds to consider the plan to drop explosives on the MOVE house, he assumed the water cannonaded onto the roof had washed away the gasoline. The leaders, at the site of a battle that endangered a densely populated neighborhood, hundreds of police and firefighters, and at least six innocent children, claimed they did not know what their boss and their subordinates knew about the gasoline. The channels of their bureaucracy failed them, their memories failed them, or, in the rush to win a victory, their humanity failed them. As a result, they were not impressed by the magnitude of the danger to life when gasoline and explosives are part of an equation that includes fire.

Inspector John Tiers, who did know about the gasoline, was standing on 62nd Street just south of Osage at 5:45 P.M. when Deputy Fire Commissioner Frank J. Scipione asked him, "Do you want us to turn the squirts on?"

"No," Tiers replied.

When Tiers was confronted with Scipione's testimony, he denied making that reply. Despite Tiers' denial, Scipione reiterated, "I'm positive that Inspector Tiers, to the question that I asked him, responded 'no'."

Fire Commissioner Richmond corroborated Scipione's recollection. He testified that Scipione reported to him that Tiers said he did not want the squirts turned on.

While Deputy Fire Commissioner Scipione was talking to Police Inspector Tiers, Fire Commissioner Richmond ordered Engine 57 to prepare to put water on the fire. Firefighters positioned a 3½ inch hose and connected it to the pumper which fed a deluge gun. The deluge gun was set up at 62nd and Osage. It fired a heavy stream of water, but it could not reach the MOVE house. As firefighters described it, "There was water at the gates," which meant they were prepared to turn on the water.

Any confusion about whether there was a fire on the roof of the MOVE house was ended by 5:50 P.M. when Lt. Powell radioed from the helicopter that he saw fire on the roof. Brooks made the same report on the radio at about the same time. However, the fire department and the police department could not communicate with each other. Brooks had a police radio but did not have a fire department radio; therefore he could not talk directly to the fire commissioner.

Mayor Goode watched the operation on a television set in his City Hall office, and his only means of communication was by telephoning Brooks at Walnut Plaza or by summoning him to a telephone with a "beeper."

In the critical period between the dropping of the bomb, at 5:27 P.M. and the end of the incipient fire, which could have been easily extinguished, at 6:15 P.M., confused communications among the mayor, Brooks, Sambor and Richmond insured the tragic outcome. The mayor saw the fire on television about the same time Powell and Brooks reported it on the police radio. The fire commissioner didn't see it, and he did not hear either report. The mayor watched the fire burn for about five minutes before he told one of his staff to get Brooks on the telephone.

Brooks was trying frantically to contact Sambor on the police radio. He also ordered his bodyguard, Police Officer Louis Mount, to try to radio Sambor. When he couldn't contact Sambor, he tried to call the fire department's communications car "F-1" with the hope it could relay a message to the fire commissioner. He couldn't reach F-1.

After eight minutes, during which the fire spread across the roof and began to impinge on the bunker at the front of the house, Brooks got Sambor on the radio and said, "We have accomplished a mission of penetrating the roof the face of that bunker is now on fire. Why don't we put the fire out?"

It was about 6 P.M. when the mayor contacted Brooks by telephone and gave what he considered to be his first order of the day: he told Brooks to put out the fire. Brooks replied that he had just given that order to Sambor. Neither of them spoke directly to the fire commissioner before 6:15 P.M.—the last clear chance to extinguish the fire.

The fire department didn't wait for an order to play water from the deluge gun onto the roof of the house adjoining the MOVE house on the east. It was as far as the deluge gun could reach. After the mayor called Brooks, he thought he saw water sprayed on the fire; therefore he did not follow up on his order. He later surmised that what he thought was water must have been static interference on his television screen. It also could have been some of the water from the deluge gun which pushed across the roof of 6219 Osage and lightly sprinkled 6221.

After about three minutes the deluge gun was turned off when Deputy Fire Commissioner Scipione ordered the men operating the gun to move it to a telephone pole where they would not be in the line of possible gunfire from the MOVE house. No gunfire was reported at that time.

Fire Commissioner Richmond believed Sambor and Brooks were in charge of the operation even after the fire began. He had previously ordered his men not to take any action to extinguish the fire at the MOVE house without the approval of a police official.

There was a small wall on the east side of 62nd Street north of Osage. Richmond was standing near the wall. Sambor approached him and they sat on the wall to discuss the fire. Richmond was certain the time was no earlier than a few minutes after 6 P.M. and no later than 6:12 P.M. Richmond said to Sambor, "What are we going to do about the fire?" According to Richmond, he asked that question when the fire could have been easily extinguished, as it was developing slowly. His recollection was not consistent with contemporaneous reports about the development of the fire.

According to the notes of Detective Stephenson, at the time Richmond asked Sambor what they were going to do about the fire, it had spread to the front of the house with ten foot dark orange flames. At 5:52 P.M., a television news reporter announced that there was a free-burning fire visible on the roof. At 6:10 he said the fire had spread down a couple of houses.

"Can we control the fire?" Sambor asked Richmond.

"I think we can," Richmond answered. Richmond believed they could control it by containing the spread of the fire.

"Let's let the bunker burn to eliminate the high-ground advantage and the tactical advantage of the bunker," Sambor said.

"Okay," agreed Richmond.

With the concurrence of the fire commissioner, Sambor walked across 62nd Street to where Scipione was standing and asked, "Can you put water on the roofs of the houses on either side."

"Yes," Scipione replied.

"Well, then, go ahead."

Scipione understood Sambor to direct him to put water on 6219 and 6223 Osage. Since the deluge gun could not reach 6223, he understood his orders to mean turn on the squirts.

It was 6:30 P.M., a little more than an hour after the bomb was dropped, and half an hour after the mayor ordered Brooks to "put out the fire," when Scipione was allowed to order firefighters to put water on either side of the blaze at 6221 Osage.

Sambor and Richmond agreed to prevent the spread of the fire beyond the MOVE house. They did not intend to try to extinguish the flames which engulfed 6221 Osage. Once the fire grew beyond its incipient stage, playing water from above the fire forced it down into the buildings. The squirts directed water from above the fire. Therefore, once the fire penetrated the roof and burned down into the buildings, it had to be fought from in front of the buildings and from within them.

Fear of gunfire from the MOVE people prevented fighting the fire with anything but the squirts and the squirts could only make the fire worse after 6:15 P.M. Just before the squirts were turned on the fire on either side of the MOVE house, it was intensified by the explosion of another gas can on the roof which added fuel to the flames.

The squirts were turned on for seven minutes, then they were turned off for six minutes, then they were turned on for seven more minutes, then they were turned off again. Each time they were turned off, it was done on the orders of police commanders who complained that steam and smoke, resulting when the water contacted the heat of the fire, interfered with the visibility of police.

Poor visibility increased the danger that armed MOVE members might escape their house and attack police from other houses. Failure to fight the fire increased the danger to the children in the burning house. There was a clear choice between the danger of death or injury to police and firefighters and possible death or injury to the children and adults in the MOVE house. The fire commissioner understood that such a choice had to be made. He was questioned on this matter during the investigating commission's hearings: "In other words it seems to me there was a choice here. And the choice was between visibility and 'X' amount of danger to the people who were in the house that was burning. I just want to know if that was considered and what was the estimate of the amount of danger to the people in the house?"

Commissioner Richmond replied that "I think to properly respond to that question, on your right hand you also have to add the danger to police and firefighters . . . It was a judgment decision, as I say, I will have to live with. I have a set of regrets on one point, and that is the four children which I have grieved very, very greatly for. But on the other hand, I don't have the other set of regrets to face and that is the death of a police or firefighter, sir."

Richmond said he understood that, "except for the fact that they had the ability to exit," the fate of the children and others in the house was sealed when the fire department did not fight the fire. Richmond's assumption that the occupants could have escaped the burning house, but failed to do so, is at odds with what happened in the dark alley behind the house at about 7:30 P.M.

Brooks remained on the ninth floor balcony after he ordered Sambor to extinguish the fire. He saw the steam and smoke billow upward when the squirts were turned on. When the water was stopped he decided to go to Osage Avenue and talk directly to Sambor. He turned to his bodyguard and said, "Let's go for a walk." They walked south on 62nd Street toward Pine. They saw the fire spreading rapidly and felt the intense heat. When they reached the middle of the 6200 block of Pine Street, the front of one of the houses near them exploded. The bodyguard quickly pushed Brooks into another nearby house as a safety precaution.

Brooks used the telephone in the house to call Mayor Goode. He also contacted Sambor to try to determine why the water had been stopped. When he left the house he met and spoke to Richmond. It was his first direct conversation with the fire commissioner since the inception of the fire. It was almost two hours after he had ordered Sambor to put the fire out, and it was almost two hours after the mayor had ordered him to put the fire out.

He encountered Richmond near 63rd and Pine Streets. The fire was raging on Osage Avenue and threatening surrounding streets. The water was off, then on, then off again. Brooks did not know why Richmond was not fighting the fire. They were two of the leaders of a failed operation that was on the brink of becoming a major disaster. Richmond had not been told by Sambor that Brooks ordered them to put the fire out. He was a career firefighter who worked his way to the highest rank in the fire department. He spent most of that evening waiting for police officers to tell him he could fight the fire.

Richmond and Brooks had worked together on other major fires during the first seventeen months of the Goode administration. There were political overtones to the MOVE challenge. There were children inside the burning house. Hundreds of people would lose their homes and irreplaceable possessions.

Despite the tense situation and the desperation they must have felt as the furious flames destroyed more and more of the neighborhood, both men recalled their encounter as brief and cordial. Richmond recalled that Brooks said, "Bill, we have got to do something about this," and that he replied, "we're doing all we can."

Considering the circumstances, both men displayed enormous restraint and mastery of the understatement. Others who claimed to have overheard the encounter recollect it differently. Brooks, they recalled, almost shouted that the fire department had let the fire burn too long before attempting to put it out. Richmond was said to have shouted back, "If the police had let us fight this thing an hour ago we wouldn't have this situation."

The fire was not Brooks' only concern. The crowd behind the barricades at 61st and Pine Streets had grown very large and more restless as the day wore on. When the flames became visible to the spectators and the firefighters did not fight them, the mood of the crowd erupted in an explosion of anger. They were shocked by the bomb. They smelled the fumes from the burning roof. They saw the fire grow until dark orange flames were jetting upward and thick, black smoke spiraled toward the evening sky. They heard the cracking, hissing sounds of fire on a rampage. They feared the children in the MOVE house would burn to death. They had viewed all of the police actions as deadly threats to the children. Throughout the day they complained and grumbled individually, but the unrestrained fire unified them. They shouted curses at the firefighters who did not fight the fire and also at the police who restrained them. They began to chant, "Where's the water where's the water?" There was no water, and the fire grew hotter and larger and more terrible. They could not contain their anguish, and they began to shout, "Murder murder." It was all they could do. It was their protest of the atrocity they witnessed. It was their prayer for deliverance from a nightmare that was not a dream. They felt impotent and trapped: trapped by city authorities with the power to suppress and restrain them; trapped by circumstances which cruelly lured them to witness a re-enactment of the worst versions of their history. Their black children and brethren were being burned alive by white authorities. It was a context that over- whelmed every contradiction of the racial dimension of the con- flagration. It no longer mattered that the mayor and the managing director were black. It no longer mattered that their fervent support had lifted Mayor Goode from a sharecropper's shack to City Hall. Only the burning children mattered. Only the agony of their history mattered. They saw only white police and white firefighters letting black children burn to death.

There is no emotional pain which is more searing, no anguish more frustrating and no injustice more demeaning than bearing witness to racial oppression. It is beyond intolerable; it is in- describably despicable. The crowds could not reach the firemen and the police, but they could reach the white sightseers who had wandered into the neighborhood to watch the spectacle. Black youths began screaming threats and attacked the whites. The youths attacked with the same racially oppressive fury they deplored. Once more violence reduced the violent to a common level. When Brooks walked to 62nd and Pine, he passed within one city block of the largest and most hostile crowd of spectators. He heard their angry shouts and curses. He heard their chants and he realized their mood could turn riotous. One of the telephone calls he made from the house on Pine Street was to Bennie Swans, Executive Director of Crisis Intervention Network (CIN). Swans' organization had a contract with the city to supply effective non-governmental intervention to allay serious neighborhood con- flicts.

Brooks told him the crowds at the scene were becoming riotous, and the police were not prepared to handle a riot. He told Swans to come to the scene to help calm the crowds. Swans contacted 25 of his workers, and they met at the police barricade.

Swans was a stocky black man who returned from the Vietnam war and was forced to help his neighbors fight juvenile gangs who fought gun battles on the streets. Ten years earlier he was one of the founders of Crisis Intervention Network. He organized teams of young black men who could mediate gang disputes and direct the gangs away from violent confrontations. CIN's success won the organization and Swans a national and international reputation. He had tried to negotiate with the MOVE members and with their friends and relatives to avoid the confrontation. On the morning of May 13, he was still trying to find a solution. He talked to relatives of Conrad Africa, one of the leaders in the MOVE house, and contacted Mayor Goode to have them taken to the scene for another effort to persuade the MOVE people to talk rather than fight. But the mayor's office did not follow through on the mayor's commitment to transport the relatives to the scene.

After the bomb was dropped, Swans knew all hope for negotiations was destroyed. He was at home, receiving telephone calls from frightened and angry residents of the Osage area, when Brooks summoned him. He dispersed his workers to try to calm various segments of the crowds. It was not easy to confront hostility that grew deeper with every breath of the fumes from the fire. It was not easy to ask people who knew and trusted them to watch calmly as the fire consumed their neighborhood and the lives of the children and adults inside the burning house. It was not easy for the CIN workers to place themselves between angry youths, attacking every white person they could find, and the helpless victims of the attacks. None of it was easy, but they did it. They expended some of the reservoir of trust which had accumulated over the years. They cajoled and persuaded and pleaded. They reminded angry spectators that a riot could result in the police turning their automatic weapons and explosives on the crowds. A riot could spread the catastrophe faster than the fire.

They escorted thirty white sightseers from the area and intercepted others before they could get there. They provided safe conduct through the crowd for white news reporters who also became targets of the racial anger. Somehow, despite the spreading fire and the growing realization of the death and destruction that would be found in its ashes, they calmed the crowds.

Swans was at the center of their efforts. He perspired freely as he talked and worked to push back the tide of anger. His efforts were interrupted by a message that the mayor was calling him on the municipal radio. Mayor Goode told him, "Bennie, I understand your people are not doing all you can do."

Swans knew the mayor was calling from his City Hall office and that his own workers were risking themselves in the midst of the angry crowds. He knew the mayor could see the fire on television, but he was on the street where he could smell it, hear it and feel its heat as well. He controlled the sudden rage he felt and asked the mayor for a telephone number where he could return the call. He did not want to express what he felt in the presence of others. As Swans went to find a telephone, the firefighters were sending for help. At 6:54 P.M. the first alarm was struck to summon additional firefighting equipment. At 7:25 P.M. the second alarm was struck. More equipment came but the fury of the fire continued to grow. At 8:02 came the third alarm, and three more were struck by 9:34. It was a six alarmer when the fire was declared under control at 11:41 P.M.

It was under control, but still burning. Before the fire died, it destroyed all the houses in the 6200 Hundred block of Osage Avenue, as well as those on the south side of the 6200 Hundred block of Pine Street whose rear yards shared an alley with the houses on the north side of Osage. Sixty-one homes and their contents were reduced to ashes. About 260 people were homeless and without their most cherished possessions.

It was a ghastly irony. The Osage Avenue residents were victims of the police from whom they expected protection. They had been assured that by nightfall they would return to their homes. By nightfall their homes were ashes. The few belongings they hurriedly gathered when they were evacuated and their memories were all that remained. Some of them wept. Some of them stood in bitter silence. The decision to let the bunker burn had dramatically changed their lives, but that decision wrought its deadliest consequences on the MOVE house. Among its ashes were found the remains of four men, two women, two boys and three girls. The children were innocent victims, and the death of the adults precluded their defenses to accusations made in the arrest warrants.

4

DARK ALLEY

Fire Commissioner Richmond had one thing right; once the fire developed beyond its incipient stage, the MOVE family had to leave their house or perish. According to the testimony of Birdie Africa, the only child to survive the fire, all of the adults and children were alive and in the basement garage after the bomb exploded. The garage door opened onto the rear yard. Beyond the yard was a driveway which was elevated about four feet above the rear alley. Their path to safety was across the yard, over the fence and onto the driveway. They could go east or west to alleys which were perpendicular to the rear alley, then north to Pine Street.

Some of them were prevented from escaping the fire; some of them made it out of the house and into the yard, but their bodies were found among the ashes of the house. Some of them never attempted to leave. Their fate was inextricably woven into the fabric of confusion and conflict which authored the tragedy. MOVE adults awaited their deaths with the traditional resignation of religious martyrs prepared to relinquish their lives for their convictions. City officials predicted peaceful enforcement of the law with a naivete approaching fantasy. Their conflicting perceptions and purposes were irreconcilable; nevertheless, concerned community leaders tried to mediate a settlement that would prevent bloodshed.

One of the leaders was Novella Williams, president of a West Philadelphia-based community organization, Citizens for Progress, for more than twenty years. She lived about seven blocks from the MOVE house. Her short, obese physique; smooth coffee-colored complexion; proud bearing and warm, welcoming smile were well-known throughout West Philadelphia. She aroused and organized her neighbors to oppose drug trafficking and street crime. She helped to persuade local banks to open branch offices in West Philadelphia. She developed day care centers for working mothers and supportive services for senior citizens.

She began talking with residents of the 6200 block of Osage, and MOVE members, about a week before the confrontation. On Sunday afternoon, May 12, she was still talking to them. She spoke to Theresa Brooks Africa, who was sitting on the front steps of the MOVE house. Mrs. Williams pleaded with Theresa to tell the other occupants of the house to surrender to the police. She expressed her fears that there would be loss of life and harm to the children if there was a battle.

Theresa insisted that the only important issue was the freedom of the imprisoned MOVE members. She claimed they were not guilty of the crimes for which they were imprisoned, and their unjust separation from their families was itself a crime. As Mrs. Williams spoke with Theresa, three helicopters circled above the street. They were flying so low that Mrs. Williams saw the pilots and the passengers. Theresa noticed the helicopters and said, "We are not afraid. We can see them trying to intimidate us. We know what they are going to do. They are going to drop something from the helicopter on our roof and then come in through the back door."

Mrs. Williams told Theresa that she did not believe the police wanted to harm the MOVE members, but they wanted to remove them from the house.

"Are you kidding?" Theresa replied. "They're coming to kill us . . . that's why they're coming. They don't want any of us left alive."

Mrs. Williams next tried to persuade the Osage neighbors to withdraw their complaints against the MOVE family. She spoke with Howard Nichols who lived directly across the street from the MOVE house. She warned that a confrontation might produce results the neighbors did not intend. She recalled that Nichols replied, "We forced the Mayor to get off his ass and do something."

"You shouldn't put this kind of pressure on your neighbor," she said.

"Will you kindly get away from the front of my door. This is a dangerous situation," Nichols replied.

Mrs. Williams understood the danger. After talking to both sides in the controversy, she understood there was little hope for a peaceful solution. Her last option was the mayor. She had worked with him throughout the years he was a community activist for better schools and better housing. He knew of her commitment, and she knew of his ability. She was proud of her relationship with him, and she had confidence in him. She was certain that as a black man with the power to take control of a situation he would not want black children killed. When she got him on the telephone, she told him the situation on Osage Avenue was very volatile.

"I don't like what I believe is going to happen. I ask you now to call it off. Don't go in there . . . we are talking to the MOVE people and I believe we can prevent this thing from happening. Mr. Mayor, we can wait a couple of days," she said.

"I've had people talking to them already," the mayor said.

"But you didn't have me. I believe there is another way, Mr. Mayor. I don't want to see those people killed . . . . Mr. Mayor, don't kill them. We have experts at getting them out of there."

The mayor told her he had consulted with the best experts in the country and he had been assured no one was going to get hurt. "You know me, Mrs. Williams. I have worked too long as a humanitarian to want anything to hurt or kill anyone. Tell me what would waiting or not going in there do to help the situation?" he said.

Mrs. Williams argued that as long as there was communication with the MOVE family there was hope for a peaceful solution, but the mayor remained convinced that no one would be hurt. He told her the city had to do something about the problem and once the public knew all the facts they would appreciate what he was trying to do.

Mrs. Williams would not concede. "Mr. Mayor, if the police go in there on the MOVE residence somebody is going to get killed. You have no control of the situation of the nature such as this. When you have a police department who are hostile to this group you have no control over their emotions and minds relative to this group. I beg you not to go in there and please don't kill them," she said.

The mayor replied, "No one will get hurt, Mrs. Williams, and I appreciate your call."

In a final plea she urged, "Mr. Mayor, you're a Christian and I'm a Christian. I beg you not to kill them and don't go in . . . I love you." She knew there was no higher authority in the city than the mayor. She remained certain a tragedy would be the inevitable result of police action. She talked to ranking police officers. She asked them to stop the operation, but they told her no one could stop it. She again went to the MOVE house. This time she spoke with Ramona Africa, who reiterated what Theresa had said earlier. They wanted nothing less than the freedom of the imprisoned MOVE members. While Mrs. Williams was talking to Ramona, a teenage child ran from the MOVE house to look at a low-flying helicopter which apparently had frightened her. Ramona consoled the child, and she returned to the house.

Once more Mrs. Williams tried to persuade ranking police officials to delay their action. Police were setting up sandbags and unloading boxes of ammunition. She saw trucks from the Philadelphia Gas Works and workmen digging trenches. She saw police carrying shotguns, automatic weapons and heavier weapons. She saw the neighborhood converted into a war zone. She was told the police would clear the area immediately around the MOVE house at 10 P.M. At 9:30 P.M. she knew it was hopeless. Nothing could stop a bloody battle and its terrible consequences, but it was Mother's Day and, as a mother, she had to try one more time.

Her daughter was concerned about her well-being and her safety, and she accompanied her when she went to the MOVE house for the last time. During their earlier conversation, Theresa told her the MOVE family wanted her to deliver a letter to the mayor and the governor. Theresa asked her to return for the letter because they needed time to draft it and to copy it by hand. She went to the house for the letter and to try once more to persuade them to surrender. Theresa met her and said, "We're not going to give you the letter we had for the governor and the mayor because it would be useless. We know the police are coming to kill us tonight . . . so the letter would be of no consequence."

The finality in Theresa's voice stifled the plea Mrs. Williams wanted to make. The hours of trying, pleading and praying for a peaceful end to the confrontation had sapped her vitality. The hope which motivated her faded, and the chill of disenchantment made her shiver. She stood behind the police barricades as it started to rain. It was a cold, soaking rain; it was not the night she thought she would have on Mother's Day. It was the one night in her life when she would bear witness for all that motherhood means. It was the night when she expended her last ounce of devotion to preserve the human life which mothers author.

She could not prevent the tragedy, and she could not leave her post of maternal duty. She stood at the barricades, in the rain, all night. She was there when the police assault on the house began. She heard the gunfire when ten thousand bullets were shot

into the house in less than ninety minutes. She heard the explosions when police tried to breach walls on each side of the
house. She saw the fire department directing tons of water at the
house, and she could smell the tear gas. It was 7:30 A.M. She was
standing in the 6100 block of Pine Street, about a block away from
the MOVE house, when she heard an explosion that was so
powerful it shook the ground. That was the explosion that tore
away the front porch and most of the front wall of the house.

Mrs. Williams went home at 11 A.M. and returned at 12:30
P.M. She remained at the barricades until 4 P.M. when she again
went home. She was at home when she heard the bomb explode.
She returned to the barricades and saw the MOVE house on fire.
She began asking firefighters why they were not fighting the fire,
and they told her they had orders not to do so.

The fire quickly became what she described as a "furious
inferno." That was when she heard gunfire from the area of the
alley behind the MOVE house. Police shouted that spectators
should get off the street. They said there were MOVE members
"loose in the area." When onlookers ran, she told them there was
no need to run.

"You see that fire over there . . . there's no way possible for
anyone to come out of that fire. They will be burned alive," she
said.

The heat inside the burning house exceeded two thousand
degrees. The women and children sat in the basement garage
under a wet blanket. They had been in the basement all day. Water,
which had been poured into the house, flowed slowly into a drain
in the garage floor, but its residue was boiling. The women—
Rhonda, Ramona and Theresa—and the children—Birdie, Tree,
Netta, Tamasso, Phil and Delicia—had not eaten that day. They
trembled in fear as thousands of bullets smashed into the house
and it was shaken by explosions. They were huddled, cringing
under the wet blanket, when they heard the cataclysmic explosion
of the bomb. The women pulled the children closer to them, and
the children began to cry. They were certain they would die that
day.

The women had chosen to follow the teachings of John Africa
to whatever end his discordant philosophy decreed, but the
children had not made that choice. According to Birdie Africa, the
children longed to live as other children lived. They wanted to eat
cooked food, to watch television and ride bicycles. They wanted to
go to school. They wanted to sleep on beds.

Sometimes, in those moments when they were left to them-selves, they talked about leaving MOVE. They talked about living without the limitations imposed by the teachings of John Africa.

Birdie was 13 years old when he lived through the most terrifying day of his life. His mother had taken him into the MOVE family when he was two. Except for the year he lived in a foster home in Virginia, while his mother served a jail sentence, he had been reared in strict compliance with the teachings of John Africa. His stay in the foster home was not a respite from the arduousness of his life because he was forced to live in a basement with several other children.

Birdie enjoyed the watermelons, mangoes and sweet potatoes that were the staples of his diet. He also liked the raw fish. The only other meat he received was one meal that included raw chicken. He did not like the raw chicken. The adults were not required to eat raw food because they had become accustomed to cooked food. The teachings of John Africa decreed that children should not be contaminated with cooked food because cooking food was not natural. Whatever the intended benefit of raw food, the children longed for the food they smelled cooking in the house.

Birdie said that one of their greatest acts of disobedience was to "sneak cooked food" when they could no longer resist its aromas. It was a violation they committed with trepidation because, if they were caught, the punishment was a meeting. The teachings of John Africa forbade spankings, but the children feared a punish-ment meeting more than they feared a spanking. During a punish-ment meeting the erring member was the target of admonishments and insults shouted by the group. The castigation and humiliation were merciless, and the children returned from the meetings crushed and crying.

Just before the bomb was dropped, the men—Conrad, Raymond, Frank and John Africa—joined the women and children in the basement garage. They heard the helicopter approach and surmised that a bomb would be dropped on the house. The explosion shook the entire house, and the children began to cry in terror. After the explosion the men returned to the upper floors until it was clear the fire would consume the house. Conrad Africa told the children it was time for them to leave the house. Smoke accumulated in the garage, and the heat became more intense. Birdie and the other children believed they were about to die. Despite the deprivations imposed upon them, there was a bond of love for the adults. The children refused to leave them. Only after the adults assured them they would see each other again did the children agree to leave the burning building. Conrad Africa unbolted the door to the yard and shouted that the children were coming out. Conrad picked up the youngest child, Tamasso, and told him to hold tightly to his neck and to wrap his legs around his waist, then he crawled out of the garage door on his hands and knees.

As soon as he crawled into the yard, Birdie heard gunfire which he described as "a 'do-do-do-do-do-do' like that. Like going off—like bullets were going after each other." The gunfire forced Conrad back into the garage. Tamasso was crying, and Conrad gave him to Theresa, who tried to comfort him. As the fire got hotter, and debris fell into the basement, the men decided the children should make another attempt to leave. Again they shouted, "The kids are coming out."

The crying children joined in shouting that they were coming out. Theresa gave Tamasso to Rhonda, and Tamasso stopped crying. The smoke in the garage was so dense that they could not breathe. Birdie saw Rhonda place Tamasso on her lap, lying on his stomach. She patted his back. Tamasso whimpered once and then was silent and still.

They knew their only chance for survival was in the yard. The heat was so intense that Birdie saw Phil's skin appear to melt as he ran out of the garage ahead of him. Ramona went out first, followed by Tree, Phil and then Birdie. Birdie was certain Phil and Tree left the garage ahead of him.

Burning debris fell into the garage and into the rear yard. They had to run through flames from the house and from a tree in the yard to get to the fence. In the yard they could hear the roar of the fire as it swept through other houses. They could hear the shattering of windows breaking and the reports of unused ammunition exploding because of the heat.

Birdie did not know whether Netta and Delicia had escaped the house, but he saw Ramona climb onto the driveway and then help Tree and Phil to safety as well. As he stumbled toward the fence, he thought he saw Tree and Phil run westward down the rear alley toward Cobbs Creek Parkway and then turn north into the alley that led to Pine Street. Ramona extended her hand and helped Birdie climb out of the yard onto the driveway. He slipped and fell into the alley. Exhausted and weak, he staggered toward the west end of the alley. Water had accumulated in the narrow alley, and it reached his chest. Pushing through the water sapped his strength and he fainted.

When police warned onlookers that there were MOVE members loose in the area, they were responding to a report on police radio that someone escaped from the rear of the MOVE house. That report was made when Conrad tried to leave the garage carrying Tamasso. The report sent police scurrying to their assigned positions to prevent an escape. The western end of the rear alley, behind Osage Avenue, intersected with an alley that extended north to south behind houses on Cobbs Creek Parkway. The eastern end of the alley intersected with an alley that extended north to south behind the houses on 62nd Street. Officers James Berghaier, Michael Tursi and Charles Mellor had reached their positions on the south side of the western end of the rear alley when Ramona, Birdie, Phil and Tree ran into the yard.

Berghaier heard a report on the police radio, "They're coming out, they're coming out, they're shooting." He heard three gunshots from a small caliber weapon. From his position behind the rear of 6245 Osage Avenue he could see the rear of the MOVE house. It appeared to him that the entire house was ablaze and flames were "rolling out of the house." He saw Ramona climb the fence behind the MOVE house and start walking toward his position. She stopped, turned and went back to try to help Birdie climb onto the driveway. She lifted him up to the driveway, but he fell down into the alley.

She started toward Berhaier again and called out, "Don't shoot, I've had enough."

Officer Mellor responded, "Keep your hands up, nobody's going to shoot you."

Berghaier saw Birdie stagger toward him. As he got closer to him, the water was deeper. Suddenly Birdie fainted face down in the water. Berghaier gave his shotgun to Tursi and said, "I'm going to get the kid."

"Watch yourself, this could be a trap," Tursi said.

"He's just a kid," Berghaier said.

The flickering light of the fire storm illuminated the narrow alley as Berghaier waded out into the water. In addition to the danger of possible gunfire from MOVE members, and police officers who may have mistaken him amid the smoke, there was the cracking sound of ruptured electric wires which flashed sparks overhead. Police aimed their guns to cover Berghaier. They were afraid that the boy, lying face down in enough water to drown, was trying to lure one of them into a trap. Berghaier's courage created a profound and redeeming moment in the tragedy. He and Birdie were more than strangers; they lived in different worlds. They were adversaries whose leaders ordered them to mistrust and to fear each other. Neither of them fully understood the dynamics of the circumstances which brought them to that dangerous moment.

They were both wet, cold and exhausted from the ordeal of that day. Conflicting ideologies did not deter Berghaier. He saw past the smokescreen of biases and mistrust to the paramount issue: his duty as a human being. Berghaier lifted Birdie from the water and carried him back toward the west end of the alley. Birdie regained his consciousness and said, "Don't shoot me . . . don't shoot me. My pants are coming down." Berghaier pushed through the water to the end of the alley. Birdie realized Berghaier was his savior and not his captor. He said to Berghaier, "I'm hungry. I want something to eat."

When Berghaier returned to his post, he noticed the stakeout officers on the roofs of houses along Pine Street. He did not know how long they had been there. The east end of the rear alley was covered by policemen assigned to Post Four, located in the second floor rear of 6218 Pine Street, and by Officers Paul Tolbert and Steve Rementer, who were in the alley behind 406 62nd Street. They were joined by Police Lt. Dominick Marandola. The alley where they stood formed a "T" intersection with the east end of the rear alley. Officer William Stewart in Post Four and Sgt. Albert Revel, positioned near 62nd and Pine Streets, had .22-caliber rifles equipped with silencers and telescopic lenses.

The fire had moved toward the east and, the heat was so intense it melted the eyeglasses of one of the officers in Post Four. Tolbert did not see anyone escape the house. He did hear Ramona shouting that she wanted to surrender. However, when investigators asked Tolbert if he heard gunfire at the time Ramona tried to surrender, he said the water cannon made too much noise for him to hear gunfire. His answer to investigators was made after his lawyer objected to the question about gunfire and said there was probably too much noise in the alley for him to distinguish gunfire from any other noise. Tolbert did hear Marandola say words to the effect that four MOVE members were lying in the driveway. Officer William Trudel was assigned to Post Four and had an unobstructed view across the rear alley into the rear yard of the MOVE house. He saw three children, a woman and a man exit the house and enter the yard.

He said he saw the man use one of the children as a shield and fire four shots from a .22-caliber rifle in the direction of Post

Four. He said the child looked petrified and was as rigid as a board. He was certain he saw muzzle flashes from the rifle and heard bullets striking the sandbags at the windows of Post Four. Trudel also saw one of the children stagger back toward the house and a woman trying to grab the child. Officer Marcus Bariana was next to Trudel. He also saw three or four people in the rear yard of the MOVE house. He saw the man with the rifle and heard him fire at least three shots. When the gunfire began, Bariana ducked down and did not see any of the people again.

Sgt. Donald Griffiths was in command of Post Four. He was lying on the floor near Trudel and Bariana. Trudel reported to him the number of people he saw in the rear yard, and Griffiths heard the rifle fire. After the gunfire stopped, Griffiths asked Trudel which direction the people ran down the alley. Trudel looked over the sandbags but did not see anyone because the smoke was too thick.

Marandola came into Post Four and shouted to Griffiths to get his men out of the building because it was on fire. Griffiths led his men to the first floor of the building where he and Trudel went to the rear kitchen. Marandola believed there were MOVE members in the rear alley. He told Griffiths to call to them and tell them to come into the building to escape the alley.

Griffiths shouted, "Come this way . . . we won't shoot." No one answered him.

Trudel and the other officers in Post Four claimed they did not return the gunfire directed at them, nor did they fire their weapons at any time when the people were trying to escape the MOVE house. The officers at the west end of the alley made the same claim.

Some of the officers heard several shots from what they believed to be a .22-caliber rifle, but, except for Officer William Stewart, they said they did not hear gunfire from automatic weapons. The police covering the alley had automatic weapons and shotguns. No automatic weapons were found among the ashes of the MOVE house. Officer Stewart was a 28-year veteran of the police department, and he was assigned as a firearms instructor at the Police Academy. He worked with weapons everyday. He had fired every weapon the police department owned. He knew the differences in their reports.

Stewart was assigned to Post Four. At the time Ramona and the others attempted to escape the MOVE house he had left Post Four because the heat of the fire became too intense. Investigators questioned him about his recollection of gunfire at that time.

Q. What time do you think it was when you had to leave
   because of the heat?
A. It was getting dark, about 7:30 P.M.
Q. Where did you go when you left your post the last time?
A. Over to the truck at 62nd and Pine Streets.
Q. Did you hear gunfire at this time?
A. From where?
Q. From the alley or driveway in the rear of the MOVE
   house?
A. Oh yes, automatic fire.
Q. Who was firing those weapons, only if you know?
A. Police officers. All the stakeout officers were running
   into the alley. They all had Uzzi machine guns.

After the answer Stewart's lawyer interrupted the interview
and took him out of the room. They returned to resume the
interview after five minutes.

Q. Did you go into the alley or driveway in the rear of the
   MOVE house?
A. Yes, but I did not shoot.
Q. Did you see Police Commissioner Sambor?
A. Yes. That's when I went into the alley. You see, I was by
   the truck at 62nd and Pine and Commissioner Sambor
   came up to me and said, 'Pumpkin, They are coming out
   of the rear of the house. Come with me.' I grabbed a
   Thompson submachine gun from the truck and ran
   down Pine Street towards Cobbs Creek with
   Commissioner Sambor and went into the alley or
   driveway in the rear of Osage Avenue. Me and the
   Commissioner started up the driveway toward the
   MOVE house and there was a burst of machine
   gunfire . . . We left the alley for safety reasons.

Sixteen days after the interview Stewart testified before the
investigating commission and said that he did not hear any police
gunfire in the alley.
   Two firemen who were in the vicinity of the rear alley heard
automatic weapons gunfire at about the time the MOVE members
were trying to escape their house. Fire Department Lt. John
Vaccarelli and Fireman Joseph Murray were veterans of Vietnam.

They were familiar with the sound of gunfire from automatic weapons. They were working near 62nd and Osage when they heard a burst of automatic weapons fire. Vaccarelli recalled that about twenty minutes later he was looking into the rear yard of the MOVE house from the second floor rear of 406 South 62nd Street. He saw at least three MOVE members in the yard.

Officers James D'Ulisse and Clarence Mulvihill were at the west end of the alley when Ramona and the others ran from the MOVE house. D'Ulisse saw two or three people in the yard in addition to Ramona. Neither D'Ulisse nor Mulvihill heard any small caliber rifle fire or saw the man that the officers in Post Four claimed had fired a rifle at them.

By the time the critical events occurred in the rear alley the fire had burned through most of the houses in the 6200 block of Osage, and fierce radiant heat threatened to ignite the houses on Pine Street. Electric wires were ruptured by the heat and they fell, some of them shooting sparks of electricity. Everyone struggled to breathe despite the thick smoke, which also limited their ability to see clearly as night fell. The only light was from the roaring flames. They were all wet and tired. They did not know when the ordeal would end. They did not know if they would survive. When the announcement was made on police radio that MOVE members were coming out of the house, each of the policemen expected to confront danger.

Firemen described the scene in the streets outside the alley as one of police running in all directions and taking defensive positions behind automobiles and trucks.

The bizarre and deadly story of the struggle for possession of the MOVE house ended in the alleys behind the house, and it ended with a mystery. The mystery was created by contradictions among policemen about how many people escaped the MOVE house and what happened to them. Perhaps the greatest contradiction was the recovery of the bodies of the women and children within the property lines of the MOVE house when there was evidence that they escaped into the yard. Despite Birdie's clear recollection that they escaped the house and ran down the rear alley, the bodies of Tree and Phil were found amid the rubble of the MOVE house. Birdie's recollection creates a part of the mystery because he recalled that Tree and Phil ran toward the west end of the alley, but the police stationed at that end did not see them.

It is not likely that Birdie was wrong in his recollection that Tree and Phil ran from the house ahead of him. His graphic description of Phil's skin melting was beyond his experience. He was not permitted to watch television or movies so he had no basis for imagining that specific description. It is likely that amid the smoke, heat and terror of his attempt to escape the fire he was confused about which direction Tree and Phil ran. If they ran toward the east end of the alley, they ran toward the officers in Post Four who believed someone was shooting at them with a rifle. The claim by officers at the east end of the alley that they either heard or saw someone from the MOVE house shooting a rifle at them creates another part of the mystery.

All of the police officers in the alley said they heard Ramona shouting that she wanted to surrender. But when it came to the question of gunfire, some claimed they did not hear any gunfire in the alley; others claimed they did. Those who did hear gunfire were certain that it was not from an automatic weapon. Only the police had automatic weapons.

Each of the police positioned in the alley said they did not fire their weapons. Even those who thought they were receiving gunfire said they did not return it. Uniformly, those who claimed they did not hear any gunfire at anytime in the alley gave as their reason the other noises around them. Those noises did not prevent them from hearing Ramona's voice.

According to the statement he gave investigators, the noises did not prevent Officer William Stewart, the weapons instructor, from hearing automatic weapons fired by police in the alleys. His later testimony that he did not hear any police firing weapons there adds an insidious dimension to the mystery.

The autopsies of Tree, Phil, Netta, Delicia, Tamasso and Rhonda, and certain physical evidence, provide proof that they did not die inside of a burning building where the temperature exceeded two thousand degrees. The remains of Tree, a 15- year-old girl, included an "abundance of pubic hair. Her body was also found with, "Levi Straus cut-off blue jeans . . . ."

The remains of Phil Phillips, a 12-year-old boy, consisted of an intact body with the hands and one foot missing. Netta Zenetta Dotson was a 14-year-old girl. Her remains included a white shirt with red trim. Tamasso Leon was a 9-year-old boy. His remains included flesh-covered parts of a body, with areas of burning, and long hair. As with some of the other remains, those of Tamasso had been commingled with the remains of dogs and other animals burned in the fire. All of his body was not recovered.

Considering the intense heat of the flames and the radiant

heat from the fire that ignited buildings across the street from the MOVE house, the hair, clothing and flesh would have been burned away if the women and children had been killed inside the MOVE house where the police claimed they found their bodies.

The remains of Delicia Africa, a 12-year-old girl, and Rhonda Harris, an adult woman, contained metal fragments. The FBI laboratory and the investigating commission's pathologist examined the metal fragments found in Delicia and concluded that they were consistent with 00 shotgun pellets. The children were in the basement garage until they attempted to escape the fire. Shotgun pellets could not penetrate the cement walls or the heavy wooden door of the garage; therefore it is fair to deduce that the pellets in Delicia's body were received outside the garage.

The metal fragments in Rhonda Harris were found by the commission's pathologist after her body was exhumed. The city's pathologist had completed an autopsy of Rhonda's body without reporting the presence of metal fragments. The failure to report the fragments and other significant aspects of the remains was typical of the violations of acceptable professional practices and procedures by the city's pathologist.

The city's pathologist was known officially as the medical examiner. He had control of the remains from May until July when the commission's pathologist began to work. During that time the remains were stored at 56 degrees, when the proper storage temperature was between 34 and 36 degrees. The remains were placed on trays and the parts of various bodies were commingled with each other and with animal bones.

One of the problems encountered during the autopsies was the dismemberment of the bodies. The dismemberment of the remains could have been caused when the building collapsed into the basement where they were found. It is equally probable that it was caused by the method used to recover the bodies from the rubble. In violation of accepted procedures, the city's medical examiner did not supervise the recovery operation from its inception.

The medical examiner rejected a request to come to the scene of the fire before the recovery began. He said that he would come after a body was discovered. Thus the police began clearing the site with a crane rather than using accepted practices similar to those used by archaeologists to prevent damage to whatever is recovered. The crane ripped through the debris, lifting human and animal remains together, and separating body parts. Once parts were dismembered it was not possible to determine whether the dismemberment was caused by the fire or the crane.

A statement made at the scene during the recovery of the bodies also helps to breach the darkness which shrouds the events in the alley when the women and children tried to escape the fire. Detective Stephenson's job of recording events continued after May 13. His contemporaneous notes of May 16 recorded the presence at the scene of Sgt. Donald Griffiths, the commander of Post Four. Stephenson's notation was, "A sergeant from stake-out is in the rear of Osage Avenue, 6221, and is pointing to an area that he states, 'I dropped an adult male from the MOVE property who fired at me when the female and child escaped'." In the left margin, opposite the notation, Stephenson wrote, "Sgt. Griffiths."

When Griffiths testified, he said he was misquoted by Stephenson. He claimed that what he really said was to the effect that the spot he noted was where one of the people dropped out of sight. Officer Trudel, who was under Griffiths' command in Post Four, testified that he was present on May 16, and he corroborated his sergeant's version of what was said.

Stephenson's notation was consistent with the recollection of Battalion Chief John Skarbeck of the fire department. He recalled returning to the scene on May 15 or 16 and overhearing a police sergeant say, "Something to the effect that I got one back there or I shot one back there . . . ."

The evidence points the arrow of logic to the conclusion that Rhonda Harris, with Tamasso in her arms, along with Ramona and the other children ran into the yard where they encountered the circumstances which sealed their fates.

As Birdie said, Ramona led them out of the garage, followed by Tree, Phil and Birdie. Birdie did not see Netta, Delicia and Rhonda leave because they came after him. The metal fragments in Delicia's body were identified as buckshot. Metal fragments were also found in Rhonda's body. If Delicia, Rhonda and Netta exited the door after Birdie, then they were the last ones to leave, and they left at the time the police were alerted to the escape. The others had gotten beyond the front of the door, but the last four—Rhonda with Tamasso, Delicia and Netta—were met by gunfire. They were felled in the yard, and that is why much of the hair on their bodies and their clothing remained.

Birdie and Ramona survived because they ran toward the west end of the alley. Since the police were standing at the west end, they would have seen Tree and Phil had they run to the west.

It is more likely that they ran east and that Birdie was mistaken about the direction. If Phil and Tree ran east, they ran toward Post Four. It was the officers in Post Four who said they believed they were receiving rifle fire. It is unlikely that they did not return that gunfire and that someone did not fire at figures running through the smoke.

The officers stationed on the roofs of the Pine Street houses were also in positions to shoot into the east end of the alley as Tree and Phil ran for safety. It is significant that every witness who heard automatic weapons fire was at or near the east end of the alley. Even if there were no sounds of gunfire, there were at least two rifles, equipped with silencers, available near the east end of the alley. Males and females in the MOVE family wore their hair in long dreadlocks and dressed in short jeans and tee shirts. Amid the darkness, smoke and steam of the rear alley, they were indistinguishable. Police on the roofs of houses looking down into the alley, and those within houses adjacent to the alley, believed dangerous felons might escape from the MOVE house. The circumstances were ripe with the potential for fatal errors.

Why were the remains found within the property lines of the MOVE house? The negligent use of a crane to search the rubble ruled out a precise determination of where they were found. If the last four people to leave the garage were shot down close to the garage door, they were lying a few feet from the spot where it was claimed they were found. Tree and Phil made it to the driveway and ran away from the yard. They must have been lying in the driveway when Lt. Marandola was overheard saying there were MOVE members lying there.

At some point before dawn's light exposed the extent of the destruction, what was left of Tree and Phil was dumped into the rubble of the MOVE house. It was dangerous to grope through the darkness to put their bodies in place—too dangerous for anyone except someone who needed to hide evidence of what happened in the dark alley.

BROKEN CHAIN OF COMMAND

Managing Director Brooks left the house at 6237 Pine Street as Ramona and Birdie were taken away in police vans. From the front porch he saw police running in various directions and shouting orders. Thick smoke drifted over the roofs of the houses and settled into Pine Street. Firefighters labored with tangled hoses in the street. He heard a report of the capture of Birdie and Ramona repeated over and over on police radio.

Confusion accelerated the pace of the disaster. He was a professional soldier who earned the rank of major general before he retired. He knew that even retreat should be controlled and orderly. He was the leader who had waited too long to try to lead. He left too many decisions to the police commissioner; it was too late to express his concerns. There was no substantive role for him, but he had to do something. He could not concede the enormous dimensions of the disaster around him. He walked among weary and tense police officers, shaking their hands and trying to encourage them. One of them told him that a woman and a boy tried to escape from the MOVE house, but police fired over their heads and they ran away toward the other end of the alley and disappeared in the smoke. At 63rd and Pine Streets he joined firefighters who struggled with hoses. He joined them and held a hose for about ten minutes. It was probably the most useful ten minutes he experienced that day. His public relations efforts with the police and firefighters didn't affect the confusion among them. They were the lowest level of command and the final repository of the confusion at the highest level of command. To the extent that

48

confusion undermines any operation, it was a primary corrosive of the plan and the operation for May 13. The mayor, Brooks, the police commissioner and the fire commissioner were at the top of the chain of command. They agreed on their objective. They wanted to peacefully arrest four MOVE members and to remove the remaining members from the house at 6221 Osage Avenue Their confusion began with the first steps they took toward that objective, and its impact on their actions increased until it resulted in chaos and destruction.

As managing director, Brooks was in charge of the city's operating departments, including the police and fire departments. At a minimum it was his responsibility to supervise and coordinate their activities. He did not have a role in planning the operation. He never saw a written plan and did not know in advance of May 13 that more than five hundred police would be sent into the neighborhood armed with automatic weapons, high explosives and an anti-tank gun. Less than a week before May 13 he did not know that would be the date of the assault on the MOVE house. He met with mayor Goode, the police commissioner and City Councilman Lucien Blackwell on May 7 when the mayor instructed the police commissioner to devise a plan for the operation. A day or two later he left the city to attend his daughter's graduation in Virginia.

The police commissioner developed the plan without communicating with Brooks. In the meeting of May 7 Brooks heard the mayor establish his policy that was to control the plan. He also heard Councilman Blackwell forcefully demand that every effort be made to avoid the loss of life, and that no police officer who was involved in the 1978 battle with MOVE, when a policeman was killed, should be assigned to the operation. Mayor Goode's policy had four major components. They were:

to pick up the children before the operation began,
to prepare a careful plan,
to proceed cautiously,
to carefully select the personnel for the operation.

Brooks left for Virginia without meeting with Sambor to determine how he intended to conform to the mayor's policy guidelines. Perhaps he thought that it was not necessary for him to discuss how the plan would be developed since Sambor received his instructions directly from the mayor. Perhaps in his order of priorities the potential danger to the Osage neighborhood was not comparable in importance to his daughter's graduation.

Brooks believed he could rely on Sambor's professionalism to develop an effective plan, but he never considered whether that reliance was a proper exercise of his professional responsibility to the city and to the mayor. He knew there was potential danger to the children in the MOVE house and to the neighborhood. He knew there was potential danger to the police and other city personnel in the operation. He knew the city had not undertaken a similar operation while he was managing director. He knew the political risks if the operation failed. He should have known that the racial composition of the neighborhood and the history of the police department with the city's black community were important considerations. Philadelphia's first black mayor instructed the white police commissioner he appointed to develop a plan for a dangerous operation, involving hundreds of police officers, in a predominantly black neighborhood.

The Philadelphia Police Department was ordered by a federal court to increase the number of black police officers and the number promoted to command positions. The Guardian Civic League, an organization of black police officers, picketed Mayor William Green, Goode's predecessor, in their efforts to force the city to adopt an affirmative action policy regarding minority police officers. Within every economic sector of the city's black community there was a firm belief in the unmitigated unfairness of the police toward that community. Placed in this historical context, racial considerations required Brooks to monitor Sambor's planning and to provide him with the guidance he needed to make certain his plans were sensitive to the character of the neighborhood and the racial overtones involved in the confrontation.

Mayor Goode's reliance on Brooks' presumed sensitivity to racial considerations was unjustified. More than one of his friends and advisors objected to Brooks when the mayor was considering him for appointment as managing director. There was no question of Brooks' professional competence, but commitment to the community was another matter. In the few years he had lived in Philadelphia he joined two organizations—the Philadelphia Chamber of Commerce and the Union League, an all-male, primarily wealthy Republican, social club.

The selection of Brooks was one of the cabinet appointments the mayor discussed with me before he made it. Brooks was not his first choice for the job. He had offered it to a very talented black woman executive, but she declined. I told the mayor that Brooks did not know enough about Philadelphia and its politics to serve effectively as managing director. He had reached the rank of major general and had run the massive army supply center in Philadelphia. In 1983, when Goode offered him the position as the city's chief operating officer, he had served in the army long enough to receive a major general's pension. His army pension was one of the reasons I cited in opposition to his appointment. I told the mayor the pension meant that Brooks did not need the job and therefore might not cooperate with him as well as someone who did. The mayor told me he was confident he could manage Brooks.

The mayor also had been warned that Sambor was not a good choice as police commissioner. Sambor was one of three police commanders and former police commanders the mayor considered for the appointment. He consulted with a former police commissioner to get an evaluation of the three candidates. The evaluation of Sambor was, "He's a flake."

Until Brooks and Sambor were appointed by Mayor Goode they were strangers to one another and did not have any substantial relationship with the mayor. They were at the top of the chain of command for the most hazardous and sensitive operation in the city's history, and their relationships were based solely on their commitment to bureaucratic channels. Each of them knew his position on the chart of the city government. Each of them knew how to accept responsibility and how to delegate it. Neither of them understood the necessity to test and compare proposals that have serious consequences. They were confident that their administrative system would produce the best result. They were also certain that relying on the system would limit their individual exposure in the event of failure.

They relied so heavily on the mechanics of management that the substance of their managerial responsibilities was forgotten, and they were confused and indecisive about critical aspects of the operation. One example of that confusion and lack of substantive initiative was the critical matter of the assignment of police. Sambor contended that he never received instructions from the mayor or anyone else to make certain the personnel involved in the May 13 operation were not also involved in the 1978 battle with MOVE members.

It was reasonable to expect that police officers who had been indicted, tried and acquitted of brutally beating a MOVE member during the 1978 battle would not be assigned to the operation.

When Brooks was asked if those specific instructions were given to Sambor, he said, "I did not give that instruction, nor did I hear that instruction given." Brooks was also asked if police who had an emotional involvement with the 1978 battle were to be excluded from the operation. He replied, "I did not say that, nor did I hear that specific statement made." Brooks participated in a meeting early in May at which the mayor claimed he instructed Sambor to select the police officers for the operation and to avoid anyone who was emotionally involved in the 1978 battle.

The mayor said he told Sambor to handpick the men. Sambor said no one told him to do so. Brooks did not hear the mayor instruct Sambor about the men, nor did he instruct Sambor. Sambor admitted that he knew certain policemen had been indicted, tried and acquitted of beating one of the MOVE members, after a policeman was killed, in 1978. That he needed an order to avoid assigning those men to another dangerous operation involving MOVE is a comment on his sensitivity. That Brooks failed to instruct him, of his own accord, is a comment on his detachment.

One result of the failure to screen carefully the police selected for the operation was the assignment of a leadership role to a police sergeant who had previously pointed a loaded rifle at the Pope when he visited Philadelphia. The sergeant was assigned as a sharpshooter on a rooftop during the Pope's visit. He was arrested by Secret Service agents when one of them, who was on the roof with the sergeant, saw him point his rifle at the Pope. The sergeant was released when he explained that he pointed the loaded rifle at the Pope in order to view him through the rifle's telescopic site.

If pointing a loaded rifle at the Pope to see him better was an indication of his judgment, what could be expected of him when the people on the other end of his weapon were objectionable radicals. Equally confused was the mayor's directive to pick up the children before the operation began. It was the most grievous break in the chain of command because there was no dispute about the mayor's order. If it had been obeyed by Sambor and Brooks, and insisted upon by the mayor, the children's lives would have been spared.

On May 7, Mayor Goode told Sambor to secure the legal authority to pick up the children in the MOVE house before the assault on the house began. On May 9, Sambor telephoned Dr. Irene Pernsley, Commissioner of the Department of Human Services. Her department was responsible for services to children.

When Sambor asked if her department could pick up children at play, she asked one question, "Are they MOVE children?"

Sambor did not tell her about the mayor's concern for the children or about the pending assault on the house. The flawed chain of command obscured critical factors Dr. Pernsley needed to consider. More devastating to the children and also to the integrity of the city's governmental operations was Dr. Pernsley's failure to inquire beyond the single question. Her dereliction of duty was the most offensive of all the faulty responses to the predicament of the children. Their well-being was her duty. All of the other actors in the depressing drama of May 13 had at least a human responsibility to prevent harm to the children. Dr. Pernsley had a professional obligation and an official duty to protect the children.

Since it was the police commissioner who asked about taking custody of children at play, Dr. Pernsley was obligated to inquire about their safety. She asked one question, "Are they MOVE children?" Once more the underlying racial considerations of the situation were ignored by a black person. She knew the MOVE children were black, she was black, and she had lived in Philadelphia throughout the years of tension between the police and the black community. When Sambor told Pernsley the children were "MOVE children," she told him there was no legal authority to pick them up unless they were victims of neglect or abuse. It was a quick and easy answer that removed any potential that she and her department would be drawn into an involvement with MOVE. Regretfully, her answer was also incorrect. In addition to neglect and abuse, the law allowed custodial care of children who were in "imminent danger." Sambor did not tell her about the jeopardy to the children. She knew about the police battle with MOVE members in 1978. The local press had reported the mounting tension between the MOVE members living at 6221 Osage Avenue, their neighbors and city officials.

Dr. Pernsley did not need Sambor to tell her the children were in danger. The indications of that danger were apparent. If she could not understand and analyze the information that was available to her, logic and instinct should have alerted her that a call from a police official about custody of children could mean the children were in danger. Her failure to extend herself to perform the duty she owed to the children was consistent with the narrow parameters of the concern for the children at every level of the planning and operation.

The mayor met with the district attorney and the U.S. attorney to determine whether there was a basis for issuing criminal warrants against any of the MOVE members living at 6221 Osage Avenue He did not meet with his city solicitor or any other lawyer to determine the legal status of the children. His failure to give the safety of the children the same consideration he gave the arrest of the adults resulted in his mistaken belief that the children could not be picked up without first obtaining a court order for their custody. That procedure would have required revealing the city's plan in advance of May 13, and that would have resulted in the children being restricted to the MOVE house.

Sambor knew that a deputy city solicitor had obtained permission from a Family Court judge to take the children into custody in advance of obtaining a court order. He did not tell the mayor. Sambor also failed to instruct police officers on duty on Osage Avenue to take the children into custody if they could do so without a confrontation. The police officers who could have picked up the children, as they traveled to and from the store with adults, were confused about their authority to act. They also did not know about the pending May 13 operation and therefore did not realize they had to act quickly if the children were to be saved.

Sambor needed supervision and guidance in processing the information he received about the children and acting to protect them. His shortcomings in that regard were manifest by his response to questioning about the responsibility he and other city officials owed to the children. During testimony to the investigating commission Sambor said he knew the adults in the MOVE house could have sent the children from the house to protect them from harm.

> Q. And, therefore, you never thought that the children controlled their status as to whether they were going to be in the house or out of the house?
> A. No, sir. Although, I might add . . . it has been brought to my attention, through one of the statements by the young man that was brought out and rescued, that he had been given that option during the day.

When he was asked if each of the children had announced from the loudspeakers that they wanted to remain in the house, would he conclude that they had made a decision they had to live with, he replied, "I had no intention of killing anyone, sir."

Sambor was then asked what his responsibility was to the

children once the battle began, and he said, "My responsibility was to, as safely as possible, execute legal process with the concerns of the health and welfare of everybody there, sir, among which were the children; but at the same time, I had to consider the safety of my personnel, and it was not we who initiated the confrontation."

Q. Commissioner, in your many years as a police officer have you ever been involved in a situation where there was legal process that had to be served, but the circumstances were such that the danger to innocent people, not the subject of this legal process, was so great that the process wasn't served and it was returned unserved because of that danger?
A. Yes, sir.
Q. Wasn't that the situation on May 13 with regard to these children?
A. It could be construed that way, yes, sir.

At best, Sambor was confused about the status of the children and the priority they deserved. At worst, he feigned concern for the children, with no actual commitment to protect them. His confusion about the status and the priority to be given the children was shared by the mayor. The mayor's failure to impose limits or restraints on the police is inconsistent with the concern he expressed for the safety of the children. Brooks' failure to intercede as the ranking official at the scene, to reduce the fire power, explosives and other violence, was inconsistent with his expressed concerned for the welfare of the children.

Prior to the 1978 MOVE battle, clear and unequivocal direction from the police commissioner was transmitted throughout the chain of command. The police commissioner determined that the children in the MOVE house involved in the 1978 battle were hostages because they could not independently decide to leave the house. Their status as hostages made their safety the first priority of the police. In 1978 the children were not harmed.

There was also better leadership in 1978. The top chain of command knew the precise legal authority for their actions. They tried to conform their actions to their legal authority. Mayor Goode, Brooks, Sambor and Richmond were only vaguely familiar with the warrants and affidavits which provided the legal authority for their actions. Their failure to inform themselves about the specifics of their authority to use force to execute the warrants added to the confusion, exacerbating the destruction of the Osage neighborhood.

Despite written communications from the district attorney, dated June 22, 1984, and May 6, 1985, advising the mayor that Frank James Africa, Ramona Johnson Africa and Conrad Africa were wanted on warrants, the mayor said he did not know of any outstanding warrants for any MOVE members prior to preparing for May 13, 1985. If the mayor, or Brooks, or Sambor had reviewed the warrants and read the probable cause affidavits upon which the warrants were issued, they would not have dropped the bomb. The affidavits contained sworn statements, before a judge, that police officials believed the MOVE members were in possession of explosives and flammable liquids. The gasoline on the roof was a major factor in igniting and feeding the fire which eventually consumed the neighborhood. Brooks knew one of the people in the house was a parole violator; Mayor Goode was told that five persons would be arrested on felony warrants, and Sambor had the same understanding. Because Sambor did not read the probabale cause affidavits, he could not tell the fire commissioner about the sworn statements that the MOVE house contained explosives and flammable liquids.

Neither did Brooks read the warrants or the affidavits; therefore he did not know if the amount of force used by the police against the house was appropriate for the violations cited in the warrants. The warrants were only accusations of crimes. All crimes are not of the same magnitude, and the amount of force used to execute a warrant must bear some relationship to the magnitude of the crime and the attending circumstances. On May 13, the top commanders had no idea which crimes were cited in the warrants, and therefore they had no idea how much force they were entitled to use. Their confusion about the legal basis for their actions was shared by the police officers who aimed their automatic weapons at the boarded windows of the MOVE house.

The police knew there was some legal basis for the assault with explosives, shotguns and automatic weapons, but they did not know if the people they sought to arrest were accused of murder or of disorderly conduct. As a result, when they thought they saw someone escaping in the alley, they didn't know if that person was wanted on one of the warrants, and if so, for which crime. None of the children was wanted on warrants, and none of the crimes alleged against the adults was a crime of violence. The police had a legal right to shoot at anyone who shot at them during the gun battle, but they did not know who fired from inside the house. They had no right to shoot at fleeing figures trying to escape the fire. They didn't know which criminal charges required them to surround the MOVE house because Sambor didn't know, because Brooks didn't know, because the mayor didn't know.

The broken chain of command failed to inform anyone of the legal basis for the degree of force they could properly use. It also failed to establish clearly who was in charge during critical periods of the battle. Any form of combat is equivalent to making an emergency landing of an airplane which is very low on fuel. It is not the time to share the responsibility for piloting the plane; chances are there is no margin for error. One of the reasons Philadelphia crashed on Osage Avenue was confusion among the top commanders about who was in charge of making critical decisions about the fire. When Fire Commissioner Richmond was asked who was in charge of fighting the fire, he said his men were required to accede to requests from police officers to turn off fire hoses. Sambor believed he was in charge until the bomb was dropped. When he discussed letting the bunker burn with Richmond, he no longer believed he was in charge; he believed they were equals.

Richmond did not believe he was Sambor's peer when they discussed letting the bunker burn. He believed Sambor was in complete control until after 9:30 P.M. Sambor disagreed because he believed Richmond was free to fight the fire without any orders from him. Neither of them thought of consulting their bosses, Brooks and Mayor Goode, when they decided to let the bunker burn. Brooks viewed his role as that of a referee, waiting to resolve any disputes that arose between Sambor and Richmond. He was certain that after the bomb was dropped Sambor was in charge and remained in charge until "it ceased to be an attempt to make arrests and it became purely a firefighting episode . . . ."

The burden of leadership during the crisis was left to the dictates of the circumstances and the definitions of Sambor and Richmond. Brooks functioned as a referee, waiting to settle a dispute. The mayor was a distant correspondent, regularly telephoning the referee for status reports. When the mayor was asked why he did not talk directly to Sambor, he said he saw no reason to speak directly to him even though he believed Sambor was the decision-maker. Other than the early morning meeting with political leaders at his home, the mayor limited his communication to Brooks. That was a serious mistake. He should have sought advice and discussion from every qualified resource. He should have listened carefully to the unsolicited advice he received from Senator Hardy Williams and from me.

Williams made several telephone calls to advise the mayor of the reaction he was receiving. During one of the calls he again suggested that the mayor "call the whole thing off since the basic plan was not working." He told the mayor that tensions in the neighborhood were rising to a level where they could explode and create a major civil disturbance in addition to the battle with MOVE. The mayor was in his City Hall office when he heard from Williams. About the same time he received similar advice from me. I heard reports of the battle on the radio. I asked the mayor if it were true that the police were confronted by automatic weapons and a fortified bunker. The mayor confirmed that he had received reports that that was the situation.

In 1967 and 1968, when I was Deputy mayor of Philadelphia, I became familiar with the training and experience of the police department. I did not believe they were trained or equipped to overcome a fortified bunker and automatic weapons, and I advised the mayor to withdraw the police and request the governor to send the National Guard. The mayor did not act on the advice. Despite the failure of the basic plan, and the misinformation he received from Brooks, he was steadfast in the belief that his commanders in the field were experts who could resolve the situation. Rather than relent and reconsider his position, he became more taciturn. By mid-afternoon it reached the point where he announced at a press conference that the MOVE members would be removed from the house by any means necessary.

As the day proceeded from one miscalculation to another, the commanders could not see the inevitable disaster that loomed before them. Only after the roaring orange flames leaped fifty feet above the rooftops of Osage Avenue, and black smoke billowed toward the evening sky did they understand the extent of their failure. By 8:30 P.M., the mayor knew he had to salvage what he could from the disaster. He knew that his commanders were not experts. He knew much of the information they gave to him during the day was inaccurate. He knew women and children were dead, and the raging fire filled the television screens of homes throughout the metropolitan area.

There must have been a moment when he wondered why this calamity had befallen him. He was a deeply religious man. His fundamentalist religious convictions were expressed in his personal relationship with God. He proudly announced to audiences and to individuals that God directed him, that his prayers were answered, and that his faith in God was unshakable. There must have been an instant when he wondered why he was forsaken. He was a tough man. His toughness was forged walking behind a plow drawn by a mule on a farm in North Carolina where his father was a sharecropper. His toughness was honed fighting to get the education his parents were denied, and fighting to build a life few thought he could achieve. If anything could break him, he would have been broken long before May 13, 1985.

The thought of children dying in the fire was the greatest contradiction of his life. Nothing in his history associated him with so dastardly a deed. There must have been an instant when he wondered how he had come so far to fall so low. That was the instant when other men, who needed to understand the mysteries of fate to maintain their emotional equilibrium, would have crumbled under the weight of their remorse. In that instant of emotional peril, the mayor had his faith. It was all he had. In the backwoods churches of North Carolina, and within black communities in every city, fiery preachers always predicted the coming of the moment when there was nothing left but faith in God. Standing amid the splendor of his City Hall office, all of the thundering warnings that had been preached to him came true. There was nothing left but his faith in God. All he could do was pray.

The press was waiting for him, a swarm of killer bees poised to sting him and wound him. At 8:30 P.M., he stepped before their microphones and television cameras: "I stand fully accountable for the action that took place tonight. I will not try to place any blame on any one of my subordinates. I was aware of what was going on. And, therefore, I support them in terms of their decisions. And therefore the people of the city will have to judge the mayor, in fact, of what happened."

It was the only statement he could make. It was all he could do to disarm the press momentarily and to reassert his leadership position. He and his commanders were trapped in the same sinking boat. It was not the time to abandon each other.

6

FAILED CAPACITY

When the local eleven o'clock news put the tragic story of death and destruction to bed for the day with another rerun of the roaring flames, the leaders of the operation prepared themselves for the days ahead. Before dawn they realized their failures were international news. Television networks besieged them for interviews. They had authored an unforgettable disaster. The media clamor became a crescendo of questions about faulty tactics, poor communications, the abdication of leadership and the lives, turned into ashes, among the smoldering ruins. The media also focused on the sixty homeless families who needed housing, clothing and money.

Philadelphians from all walks of life answered the call to help the victims. Several warehouses were quickly filled with gifts of clothing and food. More than one million dollars was collected for the benefit of the refugees of the operation. Gone were their family photographs of deceased relatives and special moments. Gone were the special letters they had saved, and the cards they received on special occasions. Gone was the favorite sweater that fit just right. Gone was the favorite chair that waited like a patient friend to support and relax them. New houses with new things would take a long time to become "homes." They lost more than bricks; they lost the memorabilia of their lives.

The greatest loss was the dead children. The human condition is only replenished by the potential of the young. Any loss of that potential diminishes the future of the species. It was the death of the children that defined the depths of the failure. The plan failed, but more than that, the city's capacity to plan failed. The city's capacity to plan for the 1985 confrontation was established by the plan for the 1978 confrontation. One fundamental distinction between the two plans was their basis for action. In 1978, MOVE members, living in a house in the Powelton Village section of West Philadelphia, were also harassing their neighbors. The neighbors sought help from city officials, and the city's leaders obtained a court order to evict the MOVE members because of their violations of the rights of their neighbors.

In 1978, every attempt was made to avoid a gun battle. Judge G. Fred DiBona issued his order evicting MOVE members from their Powellton Village house in March. The first plan to enforce the judge's order was based on a blockade of the house. By May it was clear the blockade would not produce compliance with the order. To be effective the blockade had to prevent necessary supplies of food and energy from reaching the house. However, the children in the house were considered to be hostages and their welfare was a paramount concern. Thus police had to permit the delivery of food and other essentials to protect the health of the children. In May planning was started on an alternative to the blockade. The planners included two deputy police commissioners, chief inspectors, several other inspectors and captains who had expertise in specific areas.

A written plan was finalized two or three weeks before it was to be implemented. It was based on specific information about the interior of the MOVE house and those who lived there. It specified the duties of every major commander assigned to the operation. It was shared with the leadership of the police department and with pertinent persons outside the police department, such as Judge DiBona, who issued the eviction order, the district attorney, the city solicitor, the managing director and the mayor. The police also alerted the commissioners of other city departments whose help would be needed. The plan was based on the premise that there were hostages in the house, and therefore, every effort should be made to avoid miscalculation on either side of the confrontation. The plan also allowed for continuing efforts to negotiate a peaceful compromise. To avoid miscalculation of their intentions, the police used loudspeakers to announce why they were taking every action they took as part of the plan.

The stark dissimilarity of Sambor's planning process to the 1978 process indicates a fundamental shift in the capacity of police department planning. Rather than include the police department's top command in the planning, as was done in 1978, Sambor assigned the planning to a lieutenant, a sergeant and a very young officer. Furthermore he instructed them to update a previous plan for an assault on the Osage Avenue MOVE house, which had been developed by Sgt. Kirk. Kirk and the officers Sambor selected to update Kirk's plan were assigned to either the Police Training Unit, which Sambor headed before becoming police commissioner, or the police Bomb Disposal Unit, which was housed at the Police Academy with the training unit. Sambor assigned the critical planning work to his cronies in the department and eliminated any chance of utilizing the experience and expertise of his top commanders.

One explanation he gave for his decision was his belief that secrecy was imperative. It is hard to imagine how a plan whose implementation required the coordinated efforts of various units of the police department, the fire department and other city departments could be kept secret from the leaders of the police units and could be effective without their input. It is also hard to imagine Sambor's concept of his role as a police commissioner who could not trust his top commanders to participate in a plan to evict a small group of radicals from a house. This was not a plan to infiltrate organized crime or to apprehend some other criminal element with the wealth and power to corrupt police and other officials. Perhaps the key to Sambor's thinking was his isolation as commander of the training unit.

The training unit was housed at the Police Academy which is located in the northeastern section of the city. There was very little communication and interchange between the training unit and other units of the department. The same retired city official who advised the mayor that Sambor was a "flake" also said that he had been assigned to the Police Academy because he was too erratic to work in any of the police districts. Sambor was probably aware of the importance of the plan which had to be developed and felt too estranged from police commanders to rely upon them.

Thus the capacity of the police commanders to contribute to the plan was by-passed because of Sambor's continuing view of himself as a leader isolated from his commanders. The most perplexing aspect of Sambor's planning process, which contradicted the 1978 approach and ignored the full resources of the police department, was the speed with which he required the plan to be developed.

The Kirk plan, in anticipation of a confrontation which the Osage Avenue MOVE members had announced for August 8, 1984, was developed slowly and tested in advance of that date. On

May 3, the mayor instructed Sambor to take the necessary time to plan carefully, and to keep the managing director informed. The situation on Osage Avenue had been stagnant for months. The erection of the rooftop bunkers, which were not in existence when Kirk developed his plan, required drastic reappraisal of the tactics in the Kirk plan. The 1985 planners needed to collect all of the intelligence data which was available about the MOVE house. Nevertheless, Sambor selected May 13 as the date for the assault, which required the development of the plan in less than two weeks.

The first date Sambor selected was Sunday, May 12, but the mayor objected to Sunday because it was Mother's Day. Sambor made his decision about the date without consulting his immediate superior, managing director Brooks, who left town on May 8 to attend his daughter's graduation in Virginia. Brooks participated in a meeting on May 7, when it was decided to proceed once warrants were obtained and once the plan was completed. The next day, when he left for Virginia, Brooks believed the date of the operation was weeks away. Sambor did not try to contact Brooks to inform him of the date or about the planning. When he told the mayor of the date, the mayor contacted Brooks. Curiously, Brooks did not object to the planning proceeding without him or to the establishment of the date of the operation without his input. Equally interesting is the failure of the mayor to instruct Sambor to communicate with Brooks, or to wait until Brooks returned from Virginia. The mayor's later reliance on Brooks to provide leadership at the scene of the operation was inconsistent with his agreement to completing the plan and establishing the date during Brooks' absence.

Since the mayor told Sambor he was not interested in the details of the plan, Brooks represented the only person outside of the police department who could critique the plan and recommend changes in it. However, when the mayor telephoned Brooks on Saturday, May 11, to tell him the operation would begin on Monday, May 13, Brooks did not know what the plan was.

Brooks was the civilian control of the police, and two days before a major assault he had no idea what the police intended to do on Osage Avenue. When he was questioned about the failure of the police to notify him of their plans, he said that he would have loved to have had more notice. His critical failure was that he did not demand more notice. He did not tell the mayor that he didn't know what the police were planning. If he had done that the mayor may have been more concerned about the fact that he also did not know what the police were planning. If either of them had questioned Sambor about the speed with which he was mounting the operation, they would have learned that there was no legitimate reason for haste. When he was questioned about his decision to act on May 13, Sambor said he chose Sunday the twelfth because he knew the warrants would be prepared on Saturday the eleventh. When the mayor rejected Sunday, Sambor then selected Monday because the search warrant had to be served within 48 hours.

The availability of the warrants was not a valid reason to curtail the planning time so drastically and to exclude the managing director, police commanders and others from having an opportunity to consider and critique the plan. The arrest warrants were outstanding for months and could have been executed months later. The original search warrant could have been returned, and a new search warrant could have been obtained at a later date. There was one personal consideration which may have influenced Sambor's decision about the date. He and his wife were scheduled to take a trip to France on Friday, May 17, and they would not return for several weeks. On May 3, the mayor indicated he wanted action taken sometime during May. Sambor's options were to cancel the trip or to conclude the operation before he left for France.

The city's capacity to consider its options carefully and to prepare an effective plan was thwarted by Sambor's priorities. Further insight into his priorities, and into his character, can be derived from the fact that on Friday, May 17, four days after he led an operation which resulted in the deaths of five innocent children and left sixty families homeless, Sambor took his trip to France. He left with all of the disturbing questions about the operation unanswered. He left in the midst of his departmental investigation of critical circumstances such as the actual composition of the bomb and the identity of those who knew what was in it. The entire police department suffered under the darkest cloud of adverse public opinion in its history. The mayor was facing a political catastrophe. It was a time when the city's leaders, particularly those who had major roles in the tragedy, should have been at their posts. They should have been available to help resolve any problems resulting from the aftermath of the operation.

Perhaps Sambor did not feel any obligation to remain at his post because his immediate superiors had not shown great interest in his actions before May 13. Brooks admitted that when he returned to the city on May 12, and Sambor briefed him on the plan for the first time, he was not interested in the details. He jotted down notes about the major points of the plan and then met with the mayor to convey those points to him. Neither of them questioned Sambor about the feasibility of the plan or about how it compared to the 1978 plan. Neither of them raised the question of the safety of the children, or of how their safety was assured in the plan. They just gave Sambor his head; he took the bit and dashed headlong into a disaster. The mayor absolved himself of any oversight responsibility for the plan by claiming that Sambor informed him that the final plan would be completed at a meeting scheduled for May 11. His recollection was that Sambor assured him that leading police experts and federal authorities would review the plan at the May 11 meeting to make certain it was the best one possible.

The mayor did not send a representative to the meeting to evaluate what happened, and Brooks was out of town. If the mayor had received a report of the meeting, he would have learned that its format did not provide for discussion or evaluation of the plan prepared by a police sergeant. The top commanders of the police department, leaders of the fire department and a few federal officers were given a briefing of the sergeant's plan. The plan was limited by the sergeant's knowledge and experience, and it did not provide any alternatives to force. Unlike the 1978 plan, the May 13 plan did not consider the possibility of miscalculation by either side or the possible opportunities to negotiate which might arise. Rather than try to avoid violence by announcing in advance what the police wanted to do, the operation was initiated by an ultimatum to surrender which, predictably, the MOVE members quickly and vehemently rejected.

Sambor contended that surrender by the MOVE members would have prevented the tragedy, but he must have known, before he went to Osage Avenue on May 13, that there was no real chance of surrender. The MOVE members had been stockpiling food for weeks. They obtained an army generator to provide an independent source of electricity, and they built extensive internal fortifications as well as the rooftop bunkers. The information about these preparations was in police intelligence reports and in the files of the Department of Licenses and Inspections and the managing director's office. Inspectors from the department visited Osage Avenue, at the insistence of residents there who objected to the bunker which had been erected on the roof of the MOVE house.

By surveying the bunker from the street, the inspectors concluded that it was well constructed and did not violate the building code.

If the planners had been afforded enough time to learn about the inspection report and to interview the inspectors, they would have learned valuable information about the bunker. Police surveillance also provided important information about the MOVE house and those who were living there. However, a change in the organization of the police department, which was approved by Sambor, impeded intelligence gathering and reporting. Prior to Sambor's appointment as police commissioner, intelligence gathering was the responsibility of the department's Civil Affairs Bureau. Sambor approved the formation of a new group, the Major Investigation Division (MID), and intelligence gathering was one of its duties as well. MID was not linked to any bureau of the department; it reported directly to Sambor. In order for Sambor to receive intelligence reports, they had first to be cleared through MID. Since the planning for May 13 was secret, the officers gathering intelligence were not aware of the necessity to forward their reports to the planners.

Even if the planning had not been secret, intelligence gathering was confused during Sambor's administration of the police department. An example was the failure to disseminate promptly to the appropriate persons the information that MOVE members had hoisted a large can of gasoline onto the roof of the MOVE house. It was a gasoline can on the roof which was ignited by the bomb and which enhanced and spread the fire. The fire commissioner said that if he had known there was gasoline on the roof he would have objected to dropping the bomb.

The important information about the gasoline can was given to Civil Affairs Officer George Draper on May 2. Draper forwarded the information in an informal note to his commander, Captain Shanahan. Shanahan forwarded a memorandum, containing the information about the gasoline can, to MID on May 7. MID included the information in a report it disseminated on May 19, six days after the gasoline helped to create and enhance the fire. The police department had the capacity to gather necessary information and did gather information, but Sambor's method of administration and his insistence on secret planning made the information useless.

The inexperienced planners' penchant for secrecy also resulted in a failure of the city's capacity to provide effective communications during the operation. The police plan was based on using 150-band radios for communication. The radios did not interface with the fire department's radio equipment, and they did not allow for recording transmissions. Because the need for direct communication between the police and fire departments was so obvious, the selection of radio equipment which could not accommodate that communication had to have some other purpose.

By using radios which did not provide for a permanent record of transmissions, the planners extended the order for secrecy into the operation itself. Using 150-band radios, when that use created severe disadvantages, must be construed as tantamount to a police officer removing his name tag because he does not want to be identified. The secretive planners did not want to leave a record which would facilitate an analysis of the operation. Sambor's selection of lower-level officers, with whom he was most familiar, to plan the operation in secret, not only confounded the capacity of the police department to apply its total resources to developing a feasible plan, but their inexperience also resulted in their failure to communicate properly with each other.

Sgt. Albert Revel had the primary responsibility for police tactics. He went to Osage Avenue to inspect the site where the operation would take place and to make a first-hand appraisal of the rooftop bunker. He decided a construction crane could be used to remove the bunker. Revel contacted several construction companies, but none of them had a crane which could span the distance from a secure location. On May 8, Revel contacted Richard Geppart of Geppart Brothers Demolition Company. The Geppart Company demolished the Powelton Village MOVE house after the 1978 confrontation. Geppart testified that he spoke on the telephone with a police officer, on May 8, about the feasibility of using a crane to remove the rooftop bunker. The officer asked him to visit Osage Avenue so that he could make an assessment of the task. He did so the next day and then called the telephone number the police officer had given to him. The person who answered the telephone announced that he had reached the Police Academy.

Geppart did not remember the name of the officer who asked him about the crane, but he did recall giving that name to the person who answered at the Police Academy. The officer was not available to take his call. Geppart left his name and telephone number. He received a return call from a police officer who was not the one who had asked him to consider the job. He told the caller that for a price of $3500 he would drive a crane down Osage

Avenue and lift the bunker from the roof, provided the police fitted armor plate around the driver's seat. The police officer told Geppart that using Osage Avenue involved too great a risk, and he wanted him to consider reaching the bunker from Pine Street or 62nd Street, both of which were about half a block away from the bunker. He told the officer that if trees were removed from Pine Street, so he could situate the crane on the pavement, he would try to reach the bunker from there. He said the price for that job was $6500, and he could not guarantee the results. On Friday, May 10, a police officer called Geppart and told him his proposal was not acceptable.

Sgt. Revel was certain he talked to Geppart only once, when he had asked him to visit Osage Avenue to assess the job. Revel did not receive the return call from Geppart, nor did he receive a message that Revel had called him. Revel believed Geppart was not interested in the job until October 1985, one week before he was scheduled to testify before the investigating commission. At that time Lt. Frank Powell of the Bomb Disposal Unit, who was also one of the planners selected by Sambor, told Revel that Geppart had called back and offered to remove the bunker at a price of $6500. Powell told Revel that he informed Sambor about the offer, and Sambor said he had to get the approval of the mayor. Powell also told Revel that Sambor informed him later that the mayor had rejected the crane proposal. Officer Michael Tursi, who assisted Revel with the planning, also recalled Lt. Powell's conversation about the rejection of the crane proposal by the mayor.

Powell asserted his Fifth Amendment right against self-incrimination and refused to testify about any part of his involvement in the operation. Sambor testified that Powell did not tell him about a proposal to remove the bunker for $6500, and he never requested the mayor's consent to any such proposal. He explained that if he had believed such a plan was feasible, he could have paid for it from the police department's budget. Geppart offered the city the best possible alternative to using a bomb to remove the bunker. He was prepared to drive the crane down Osage Avenue and lift the bunker from the roof. With the bunker removed the explosives that were used on the party walls of the house that destroyed the front of the house and started the fire that burned down fifty houses and killed several people, would not have been necessary.

The explosives were employed to avoid the tactical advantage of the bunker. The opportunity to remove the obstacle that inspired the bomb was lost because one of Sambor's planners assumed too much authority in rejecting the crane proposal. Lt. Powell was the commander of the Bomb Disposal Unit, and May 13 was his first opportunity to use explosives in combat. If the crane proposal had been accepted, it was an opportunity he would have lost.

7

ANGER ON
OSAGE AVENUE

The misadventure, which culminated in the explosion of the bomb on the roof of the MOVE house, was part of the city's efforts to avert a human explosion on Osage Avenue. The explosion was threatened by the residents of the 6200 block of Osage who had reached the end of their tolerance of psychological warfare by their MOVE neighbors and of inaction by their city government.

Their threat to employ violent means to eliminate the MOVE house, to restore peace on their street and dignity to their lives, was not a sudden empty outburst.

Until their neighbors in the MOVE house declared war on them, they were proud and productive members of the community and the city. They were the working families whose greatest financial investments were in the small row houses in which their energies created homes. They were pleased to live in a section of West Philadelphia which was close to the linear park that bordered the serpentine contour of Cobbs Creek; 63rd Street and Cobbs Creek Parkway were the western limits of the 6200 block of Osage and the eastern boundary of the park. West of the creek were the suburban towns of Darby, Upper Darby and Yeadon. The park began four blocks north of Osage and stretched like a long, narrow, crooked green finger southwesterly five miles to Baltimore Avenue It gave a special quality to the neighborhood. It offered a respite from the vast grid of row houses and asphalt streets which stretched westward from City Hall. Residents could walk to the park for picnics and barbecues. Their children could play amid the grass and trees of the park everyday. They enjoyed the fresh new foliage of spring and the splendor of the trees about to shed their leaves in the fall. The park gave added value to their neighborhood.

Prior to their problems with the MOVE house, the only serious neighborhood tension was engendered by fights between black teenagers from their neighborhood and their white counterparts from the suburban towns. They had intermittent, territorial clashes in the park. Latent racial animosity, which bedeviled the generations of their parents, lingered as does a sore that is slow to heal. It was the kind of tension they had learned to live with. The same soreness lingered in their daily lives. They understood that their blackness was still not satisfactorily accepted or respected, but they knew how to live with that as they worked to overcome racial restrictions on the futures of their children.

The residents of the block who had lived there the longest knew Louise James, who purchased the house at 6221 Osage 27 years earlier. They were her neighbors as she raised her children in that house, including her son, Frank James, who became Frank James Africa when his mother ushered him into the MOVE family. Her maiden name was Louise Leapheart. Vincent Leapheart, her brother, became John Africa, the founder and prophet of MOVE. She and her sister, LaVerne, joined their brother's movement during its early years. As Louise Africa, she was often an eloquent writer and spokesperson for MOVE. Her adherence to the truth as taught by John Africa was permanent. When she left the organization, she remained imbued with the MOVE doctrine. Her son, Frank, never left the organization. His steadfastness to MOVE and to his uncle's testaments were intact when he perished in the fire.

The residents of the 6200 block of Osage knew about Louise's involvement in MOVE, and they knew that Frank was a member and that he had been in trouble with the law, but they accepted them as neighbors. The community of black people, as with other ethnic communities, reserved to itself the right to make separate judgments about its membership. The judgments of those outside the black community did not determine membership status. Blacks understood the capriciousness of bigotry strengthened by legal authority, and therefore official judgments of their members were always suspect. When Frank moved into his mother's house at 6221, he was welcomed by the residents as they would welcome the son of any other neighbor who had returned home. Lloyd and Lucretia Wilson lived next door to Louise James, in 6219. They had a friendly relationship with Frank. They discussed common interests and concerns. Sometimes Frank talked to them about MOVE and the teachings of John Africa.

The Wilsons listened and tried to understand. They had become Buddhists and knew the social estrangement of membership in a religion which was not common in America. Their friendliness and acceptance did not change as more MOVE members came to stay in 6221. The neighbors noticed the growing family of men, women and children, always dressed in jeans, with their long hair twisted in dreadlocks.

The MOVE family was different from the other families, but their differences were accepted. The MOVE members began their residence on the block as good neighbors. They sold fresh fruits and vegetables throughout the neighborhood. One of the tenets of John Africa was that God's natural law forbade cooking food. Thus the diet of MOVE members was primarily of uncooked fruits and vegetables. The MOVE principles also dictated that, as a part of nature, animals were entitled to freedom and care. The MOVE members took in a wide assortment of stray dogs and cats, and they volunteered to exercise their neighbors' pets when they took their own menagerie to the park. They later expanded upon the expression of their concern for animals by surreptitiously releasing pets from the confinement of their owners' rear yards.

The residents of the block suspected MOVE members of creating the minor annoyance when they found their pets roaming the street unattended in the morning, but they understood the concern for animals which motivated MOVE and, initially, they did not complain. They did not understand that the intrusion upon their dominion over their pets would grow into an intrusion upon their dominion over their own lives. The number and variety of animals living in the MOVE house grew rapidly. By May 13 there were about twenty dogs living in the MOVE house. The residents of Osage learned that MOVE's concern for other living creatures was not limited to cats and dogs. The MOVE house was also a haven for insects and rats.

Before the fire ended the ordeal of living next door to the MOVE house, the Wilsons were driven from their home by an infestation of insects. Mrs. Wilson was required to turn on her kitchen stove and let it heat to evict the bugs before she could cook. Even after that precaution, bugs would remain and get into the food she prepared for her family, and she was forced to throw it into the garbage. Insects covered the wall adjoining the MOVE house, and they swarmed over the windows so thickly no light could enter. Rats and insects invaded and occupied the Wilson's basement, and Mrs. Wilson was unable to use their washing machine and dryer. The Wilsons fought the vermin. Mr. Wilson recalled that many of the insects were unlike anything he had seen before, and some of them would not die or run when he hit them. When their children suffered insect bites on their bodies, the Wilsons were forced to retreat from their home.

As the situation deteriorated within the Wilson household, it also deteriorated for other residents of Osage. They noticed that the MOVE children did not attend school. In the spring of 1983 some of them saw the MOVE children eating from the garbage cans in the rear alley. They knew the MOVE adults would not accept food from them, so they began replacing their garbage with loaves of bread and other wholesome food which the MOVE children ate. The concern which residents of Osage felt for the MOVE children grew as rapidly as their consternation with the MOVE adults. They watched the environment on their block become polluted by vermin, garbage and raw meat that were thrown into the street, and by feces from dogs, pigeons and rats. They tried to discuss their concerns with the MOVE adults, but they were rebuked with quotations from the teachings of John Africa.

The MOVE house became an eyesore. Waste lumber and other debris littered the front and rear of the house. MOVE adults built a fence that blocked the rear driveway which provided access to all of the houses on the north side of the street. They also erected vending stands on the street from which they sold vegetables and fruit. The stands blocked the curbside parking spaces which certain residents had used for years. There were angry quarrels about the impropriety of the stands.

For the residents of Osage the evidence was overwhelming. MOVE's presence on their street was a spreading cancer that would eventually destroy their homes and the value of their property. The pollution was as deadly as any pollution which had ever threatened a community. Their children began to ask disturbing questions about the children and adults who lived in the MOVE house. They asked about the profanity that dominated the MOVE vocabulary. They asked about children who were not required to attend school and do homework. They asked about the rats that frightened them and the insects that were everywhere. They asked about the unavoidable stench that wafted into the street from the MOVE house. They wanted to know why their street had changed, why their lives had changed.

Each day the MOVE adults displayed greater contempt for the lives of the other residents. Each day they added to the destruction of the lifestyle which had existed on the 6200 block of Osage before they moved in. The community responded as individual citizens should respond to a threat to their neighborhood. They telephoned and wrote letters to city authorities who, they believed, had the responsibility and the power to remedy the situation. The authorities did not respond. Normally the proximity of Cobbs Creek Park made summertime a delight for the residents of Osage, but not in the summer of 1983. During the fall and winter months, their children had some relief from the MOVE influence while they were in school. When the school year ended, so did their daily respite from the MOVE presence. The children became more apprehensive. Some of them became ill from the stench of garbage, decaying meat and animal waste trapped by the hot, humid air in their small street. As the temperatures of summer rose, the tempers of the residents got hotter, and unfriendly encounters with MOVE adults became commonplace.

Verbal exchanges became more and more heated as some of the men of the street felt compelled to respond to the conditions that adversely affected their families. They tried to reason, but reason failed. They knew it was their responsibility to protect their homes. They wanted to do that within the sanctions of the law, but the lawful authorities did not respond when they individually requested them to act. They were left with basic masculine instincts. Their courage would not permit them to accept indefinitely the indignities MOVE imposed on their families. The summer heat lingered in the streets of West Philadelphia on September 24 when Wayne Butch Marshall decided he had had enough of MOVE's intrusions on his life. The MOVE adults had placed a vending stand in the street near the curb where Butch regularly parked his car. He got out of his car, moved the stand and then parked in his spot.

Two women ran from the MOVE house and attacked him. They leaped onto his back and began to scratch him and bite him. He pushed them away repeatedly until they were joined by one of the MOVE men, named Moe. When Moe joined the attack, Butch knocked him to the ground. Then Frank and Conrad ran from the MOVE house and joined in the altercation. There were too many of them for Butch, and he was knocked down and severely beaten. None of his neighbors came to his rescue. They understood his anger and his frustration. Some of them wanted to throw a punch to soothe their anger, but they were law-abiding people. They would not take matters into their own hands. They would not set the wrong example for their children.

Some of them had moved to that pleasant section of West Philadelphia from sections of the city where a propensity for violence was essential to survival. Some of them were reared in neighborhoods where they learned to fight as soon as they learned to walk. They learned to fight or be beaten. They learned to fight to gain respect. They had moved away from that lifestyle, and they did not want to resurrect it where they lived. They deserved the protection of the law, and they decided to insist upon that protection.

Their individual complaints to the police had resulted in surveillance of the MOVE house by a plainclothes police officer from the Civil Affairs Unit. His name was George Draper, and they knew him and knew why he was on their street, but he was not there often enough, and he was not authorized to take any action.

The day after the fight between Butch and the MOVE members, Gerald Africa, the MOVE Minister of Information, visited the MOVE house. While he was there a verbal confrontation erupted between him and some of the men who had not fought with Butch but felt compelled to express their support for him. They shouted curses at each other for several hours until Officer Draper interceded and ordered Gerald Africa and the other MOVE members to go into their house or be arrested. Gerald Africa told Draper that he could not interfere in MOVE's business because MOVE was beyond the law. They had indeed been beyond the law. None of the legal authorities would enforce the codes and regulations that the residents of Osage were required to obey, and which must be obeyed to maintain an organized and healthy environment. The residents decided to make an organized effort to force city officials to respond to their complaints. They prepared and circulated a petition which was signed by every household on the block. They also scheduled a block meeting to unite their efforts to obtain protection from the city.

Officer Draper reported the plan for the meeting to his commander, Captain Shanahan. Shanahan telephoned Gloria Sutton, who worked for the Philadelphia Commission on Human Relations. She was an expert in mediating neighborhood disputes, and had been active in trying to resolve difficulties between MOVE and their Powelton neighbors, in 1978. When Sutton contacted Draper, he told her the neighbors were at the boiling point. Some of them told Draper they would "take care of" MOVE if the city could not handle them. He also said that during the argument in the street threats of "We'll kill you" were made by both sides. Sutton called the MOVE house. The MOVE adults remembered her. She had helped them solve problems as she had done for other city residents. She was told that the problems with Butch and the other neighbors were beyond her help because the city had not been interested in the basic problem which was the imprisonment of MOVE members for the 1978 murder of a police officer.

Later that evening she attended the meeting at 6228 Osage, the home of the block captain, Mrs. Inez Nichols. It was a neat, modestly furnished home which, like so many other Philadelphia row houses, seemed to welcome visitors with a warm embrace. Ordinarily, she would have been immediately relaxed and at home there, but Sutton could feel the animosity welling in the twenty residents who crowded into the first floor. They presented her with a carefully delineated list of the grievances which they believed were amenable to solution. They could not articulate the deeper personal grievances they harbored. No one could heal the rupture of their lives. No one could rebuild the self-esteem which had been diminished. No one could restore the common joys which had been lost. They listed the infractions which they knew the law would not permit MOVE to maintain:

1. Open garbage bags and chunks of raw horse meat placed in milk crates in driveways of neighbors.
2. MOVE removes all animals, even pets of residents, and feeds them. They have removed flea collars from one resident's cat five times. There are pigeon coops and feeding of birds on their property.
3. MOVE has extended their yard across driveway, preventing passing through driveway. Residents recently paid $2000 per house for repaving.
4. House has approximately 13 or more children and 8 adults.
5. Vending produce (watermelons sold from property and out front). Homemade watermelon carts are parked in street and handles protrude onto sidewalk, inhibiting passing. Some carts are parked on the pavement, and residents must walk into street.
6. MOVE children are openly aggressive to neighbors' children, but on some occasions, they were disciplined when neighbors spoke to MOVE members.

7. MOVE members threatened to kill the 17-year-old son of one neighbor who threw dirt at a MOVE cat that would not leave his property.

8. Neighbors have called L&I, who referred them to Streets and Highway department, who all said they could do nothing. Fire department also unresponsive regarding violations. MOVE has built a wooden barrier around their skylight on roof, and walk up and down all roofs day and night. One resident said she looked as she sat on the toilet and saw MOVE walking up there (patrolling, not peeping).

9. At night MOVE opens all gates where residents have pets enclosed, and lets pets out and feeds them and allows them to roam the streets.

10. MOVE picks in their neighbors' trash and garbage that has been set out for collection. Police/Sanitation gives tickets to residents.

11. Clothes consistently disappear from residents' lines, and MOVE is suspected.

12. Neighbors observed two MOVE women jump on Wayne Marshall. One bit a piece from his jaw on September 24. Wayne was present and says he will file a complaint at the police station.

13. MOVE claims they will soon have a large demonstration.

14. MOVE says if anyone comes back on extended area behind their property, they will shoot their heads off.

Sutton had promised to arrange appointments for representatives of the block to meet with appropriate city departments when Iris Henderson, of 6032 Osage Avenue entered the meeting. Mrs. Henderson was a political and community activist, and the elected committee-person for that area. A committee-person is the political leader of a division, which is a segment of a ward. Each political party has leaders of the 69 wards of the city who are selected by the committee-people, and the committee-people are elected by the voters. Sutton explained that she was a mediator, and therefore she would not only meet with residents of Osage, but would also meet with and talk to the MOVE adults about their side of the dispute. Mrs. Henderson interjected that she would arrange an appointment with City Councilman Lucien Blackwell, who could help them get an adequate response from the city departments.

The residents of Osage decided they did not want a mediator, they wanted an advocate. They believed their personal attempts to settle their differences with MOVE were mediation enough They were certain that without swift and decisive action the situation would only worsen. They left the meeting with some hope but with no assurances that anything would change, and nothing did change. They continued their efforts to get some city department to take action on their behalf, but there was no response. They did not know they were victims of a policy of inaction. Every city official knew the history of official conflict with MOVE. In the aftermath of the 1978 battle at the MOVE house in Powelton Village, MOVE members were considered to be too dangerous for city inspectors and others to perform their duties without police assistance. The police believed MOVE wanted a bloody confrontation, and therefore police officers were instructed to avoid a confrontation unless it was a departmental operation.

The policy of inaction was not announced or decreed by any authority; it evolved from the bureaucratic logic that prefers the path of least resistance, and avoids controversy at all cost. The policy began during the administration of Mayor William Green, but he never developed it or condoned it. Raymond Tate, Commissioner of the Department of Licenses and Inspections in the Green administration, testified that it was his policy to avoid problems involving MOVE properties. Wilson Goode was managing director in the Green administration, and he said the policy of non-enforcement evolved during the period after he resigned as managing director to run for mayor. Former Mayor Green disputed Goode's contention about the evolution of the policy. Green claimed that it was his policy to enforce the law in all situations and particularly where MOVE was concerned.

It was not the origin of the policy, nor the responsibility for the policy which confirmed its existence for the residents of Osage—it was the effect of the policy. Former Mayor Green's disclaimer notwithstanding, while he was mayor city departments did not respond to complaints about regulatory violations at the MOVE house. While he was mayor the police department assigned Officer Draper to watch the MOVE house, but it did not respond to complaints from the residents of Osage, and it did not provide assistance to any city department seeking to perform duties at the MOVE house. Green was mayor when the residents of Osage met to outline their complaints against the MOVE adults. The complaints included alleged violations of city building codes and health regulations. Green's claimed policy of enforcement when MOVE was involved did not result in any response to the complaints. On October 3, 1983, while Green was in office, the residents of Osage delivered a written statement of their complaints and a supporting petition signed by all of the residents of the block, except the MOVE members, to the city department of health and human services. A copy of the statement and the petition was delivered to Mayor Green's office. There was no response.

There were police reports about the problems the residents of Osage were having with the MOVE house; there were direct police contacts with MOVE; there were meetings to protest the city departments' failure to respond, all while Green was mayor, and there was no enforcement. However it was transmitted to the city departments, there was a policy of inaction on complaints against the MOVE house. Mayor Goode admitted that he adopted the policy which evolved during the Green administration and that he agreed with it. He did not want to risk injury to city personnel in a confrontation unless it was the result of a planned operation. By mid-October of 1983, the residents of Osage were again at the boiling point. The hope inspired by the meetings in September had faded, and once more they believed they were abandoned by their elected leaders. On October 19, they met with Peter Truman, who was their ward leader and state representative, in his office.

They were beginning to believe their street could not be saved, and they had learned that the presence of MOVE destroyed the value of their houses, which they could not sell. Truman listened to their complaints, and he also heard the deep frustration and anger in their voices. There was less than a month to the general election when Truman was certain Goode would be elected as the city's first black mayor. That was his ace card. That was all he had to try to forestall civil violence in his district. When no other argument or assurance would calm them, he played his ace. He told them they should not do anything to endanger the election of the city's first black mayor. Some of them said that they could not live with MOVE until the election; they wanted action immediately. Most of them relented. They were required to weigh the personal misery of their families against the most cherished political goal of the black community. For more than a decade there had been one effort after another to elect a black mayor. All of the efforts failed. With every failure the determination to succeed grew stronger.

With two weeks left to the campaign, all of the polls indicated Goode would be elected. They could not endanger that achievement. Truman assured the Osage residents that very soon after Goode was elected definite action would be taken against the MOVE house. About two weeks after Goode was elected, they met again in Pete Truman's office. They expected city action to at least remove the fence which blocked the rear drive. Truman was not present at the meeting. Mrs. Henderson acted as chairman in his absence. As soon as the meeting began, they expressed their anger with politicians, and specifically with Truman, who had promised them action after the election and was not there to meet with them.

Clifford Bond had replaced Mrs. Nichols as black captain, and he had sent registered letters of complaint to Mayor Green, the police and fire departments and the managing director. He did not receive responses to the letters. Mrs. Sutton reported that Gerald Africa and Conrad Africa had met with the chairman of the Commission on Human Relations to discuss the problems caused by the fence blocking the drive. MOVE refused to remove the fence and warned that any city agencies that might try to remove it should have guns. Gerald and Conrad also stated that MOVE members desperately needed housing for about twenty children of incarcerated MOVE members. At the conclusion of Sutton's report, the residents in the meeting expressed their fear that there was no chance MOVE would leave their street if the MOVE members were desperate for housing. The anger, which charged the atmosphere in the small office, gave way to despair.

Mrs. Henderson understood the community's anger and she sensed their despair. Their despair could drive them to consider seriously the threats they had previously made to evict MOVE from their block and from their lives by their own devices. Henderson interrupted their discussion of the likelihood that MOVE's housing needs insured their continued residence in the 6200 block of Osage Avenue. She told them she was certain the city was planning some action against the MOVE house. Some of the residents said they thought that might be true since the area was under constant surveillance by unmarked police cars. Henderson quickly suggested that they exchange their telephone numbers to allow for quick communication in the event the police requested them to evacuate the block.

In December the chilly winds, announcing the coming of winter, kept most of the Osage families in their homes. Their children played indoors, and contacts with MOVE were reduced. Some of them noticed that the MOVE children continued to be about on the street, and that they did not have jackets or coats.

Despite their intense dispute with the MOVE adults, some of the Osage residents gave jackets and coats to the MOVE children. They were the clothes which remained in their closets after their own children had outgrown them. They were in good condition and they were warm. The MOVE children smiled and thanked them for the warm jackets. When they went to the MOVE house, they returned without the jackets, which the MOVE adults had taken from them.

About the middle of December the residents heard the banging of hammers at the MOVE house. They looked from their windows and saw the beginning of the fortification of the house. The men were placing wooden slats over the windows. One evening some of them heard loud shouts and screams coming from the MOVE house. The front door opened and Louise ran from the house with her son, Frank, chasing her with an ax. After her eviction the pace of the fortification increased, and large loudspeakers were installed on the roof.

As the Christmas season approached, the Osage families tried to ignore the discordant presence of MOVE. The small children were excited with expectations of gifts and toys, and the windows of the neighborhood were decorated with Christmas lights. The shopping and decorating chores of the season lessened their awareness of the MOVE house, and they hoped they could enjoy the Christmas spirit. Christmas Eve in a small row house can be one of the wondrous delights of human experience. It is one of the times when the closeness imposed by the small streets and the limited space of the houses enhances life's pleasures. Red, green, amber and white lights glistened in almost all of the windows. Some of the streets decorated by extending strings of lights from the upper floors of houses on opposite sides of the street.

Radios and record players played Christmas music as the families of the neighborhood gathered to decorate their Christmas trees. There were indications that Christmas Eve of 1983 would be another season of special joy, despite the presence of MOVE.

It was 10 P.M., just after most of the smaller children had been sent to bed, when they heard the first blast of MOVE's war. It destroyed the burgeoning joy of Christmas. The profane diatribe penetrated every home. The Wilsons' bedrooms were adjacent to the location of the loudspeakers, and the amplified voices seemed to shake the walls. The children were frightened and confused by the profane intrusion into their homes, and their parents could not console them. Several residents telephoned the police to plead for help. Surely they would respond to stop the destruction of Christmas. This time the police would be forced to act. The police operators politely recorded the information from each call, but there was no response. The policy had not changed, and it did not allow exceptions for Christmas. Some of the children wept that Christmas Eve. Some of their parents cursed the circumstances they could not change. The beauty of Christmas music was drowned out by the shrill voices hurling profanities at the residents, city officials and the "system" in general. It continued until 4 A.M. When it stopped, the spirit of Christmas had been murdered on Osage Avenue.

Goode took the oath of office in January 1984, and there was renewed hope that he would take decisive action to solve the problems on Osage Avenue. The Osage residents were too politically innocent to understand their position in the hierarchy of the city government's priorities. The city's business leaders demanded the mayor's action to revise the business taxes they paid. The unions wanted the mayor to proceed immediately to create more jobs. There was a general clamor for resolution of the political haggling which delayed the award of franchises to provide cable television service to the city's neighborhoods. The mayor had to appoint the key members of his administration, including those persons who would ultimately join in the process that destroyed Osage Avenue.

The war on Osage had to wait. Delay strengthened the resolve of the MOVE members and increased the animosity of the other residents. MOVE's threats to repulse by violence any attempt to enforce the law which governed them were substantiated in April 1984 when the city water department attempted to terminate water service to the MOVE house. Water department employees tried to enter to cut off service, and the MOVE members warned that they would shoot them. The employees then sought the assistance of the police, and the police refused to assist them. Two days later, on April 15, Louise and her sister, LaVerne, went to the door of the house and tried to enter. They were also repulsed. Louise demanded that she be given access to her house, and someone called from inside, "You don't have no fucking house and don't come in." Her son, Frank, was standing in the front door as she got into a car to drive away. Suddenly MOVE members ran from the house and jogged alongside the car, cursing her and warning her not to return.

The residents' continued demands for help resulted in a

meeting with Mayor Goode and members of his administration on May 30. The mayor was sympathetic but told them he could not take any action to evict the MOVE group without a legal basis. The residents charged that they had not received responses to their many written and oral complaints to various city departments. A representative of the Department of Licenses and Inspections, who was present at the meeting, said that she attempted to process complaints, but she was told not to bother. The mayor explained the danger of initiating a confrontation without a legal basis for taking action.

Mrs. Betty Mapp, one of the Osage residents, told the mayor that she understood there was a parole violation warrant outstanding for Frank Africa. The mayor said that he had not received that information from the parole board.

Mrs. Mapp was correct. In March a state parole agent went to the MOVE house to determine why Frank had not kept his appointments. The agent was threatened and refused entry into the house. As a result Frank was declared a delinquent parolee in May 1984 and as such was subject to arrest by any police officer.

After Frank was declared delinquent, Yvonne Haskins, regional supervisor of the parole board, notified Chief Inspector Nestle of the Philadelphia Police Department that Frank was a delinquent parolee. She requested arrest warrants for him. On June 5, Mrs. Haskins was visited by Chief Inspector Wollfinger and Captain Shanahan of the Philadelphia Police. They asked her not to try to execute the arrest warrants for Frank because the Osage Avenue situation was too explosive. The next day the arrest warrants were issued. Frank was on parole from a conviction on charges of riot, possession of an instrument of crime, and general and terroristic threats. The parole board considered him a serious offender.

Mrs. Haskins was bound by the parole board's policy which prohibited parole agents from serving arrest warrants if they would be placed in danger. In such cases they were required to obtain the assistance of the local police. The police had already told Haskins they would not assist in the arrest of Frank Africa. The arrest warrants were held in abeyance for police assistance. Thus a serious offender was permitted to violate parole while he waged psychological warfare against the families on Osage Avenue. Moreover, Frank and the other MOVE members announced that they were preparing for a major demonstration on August 8 to commemorate the 1978 battle with the police. The warrant for

Frank's arrest gathered dust as he victimized the families who were his neighbors and dared city officials to interfere with MOVE.

On July 4, the residents again met with the mayor. By that time the arrest warrant for Frank had been outstanding for a month. Nevertheless, the mayor again said that he did not have a legal basis for taking any action. His police department had not informed him of their request to withhold the arrest warrant, and he had not tried to determine if the information Mrs. Mapp gave him about an arrest warrant was correct.

The residents were encouraged when they learned the police were preparing for the confrontation that was announced for August 8. Once more they established their communication network to facilitate a quick evacuation of the street. The summer months renewed the angry encounters, and in one such encounter Mr. Wilson was attacked by Frank. The street grew tense as the early days of August passed. On August 8, hundreds of police descended on the neighborhood. The children were quickly evacuated, and adults were summoned home from their jobs. The entire neighborhood anticipated the first shot, but it was not fired. The police waited for MOVE to make the first move, but MOVE was only interested in noting the police response. Their announcement was just a test run. They suckered the police into showing how they would respond to a threat. After that they began to work day and night to improve their fortifications.

In the aftermath of August 8, the residents were furious. The police had finally come to their street in force, but they did not do anything to solve the problem there. The police left and the situation became more intolerable. The MOVE members doubled the volume of their loudspeakers and also increased the vehemence of their diatribes. The winter months again provided a respite from the contacts, but the anger on both sides of the controversy became more intense. By April 30, 1985, the residents believed they had to shoot it out with the MOVE house or find another place to live. They decided to fight for their street. In one final, desperate attempt to remain within the law they sent a letter to the governor, pleading for his help. The critical message of the letter was, "We love our block, and we will not be driven out by anyone. WE DO NOT WANT A BLOODBATH, but WE WILL NOT BE DRIVEN OUT BY ANYONE. Your office is the only thing standing between this day and a bloodbath on Osage Avenue. We are law-abiding, taxpaying citizens, sir, but we have reached critical mass."

8

THE COMMISSION

The Osage Avenue residents' letter to the governor was reported in the press, and it was clear to the most cautious city bureaucrat that delay was no longer a viable option. The city had to do something to end the torment of the hapless residents, or there would be a bloody civil war on that block. The threat of a "bloodbath" initiated the planning which culminated in the police assault on the MOVE house. The threatened human explosion, which would have embroiled the 6200 block of Osage Avenue in a gun battle between the MOVE members and the other residents of the block, was averted; instead there was the explosion of a bomb.

It was about 9:30 P.M. as I watched a televised report on the fire that swept through Osage Avenue. The commentator speculated about how many adults and children might have been killed, and how many houses would be destroyed by the fire. I knew Mayor Goode was also watching the television reports as he tried to cope with the expanding dimensions of the tragedy.

In moments of victory and success, leaders are immersed in adulation. Sincere and insincere well-wishers gather close to them and enhance the celebration of achievement. In moments of failure and catastrophe leaders are usually alone and lonely. When everything goes wrong, it's like trying to climb up out of a deep hole that has walls covered with thick lubricants. Every struggle up is nullified by a deeper slide downward. It's impossible to get away from the bottom without help, but there is no help, and no way to get a grip that will allow them to help themselves.

I telephoned the mayor's office, and when he answered the telephone, I asked him if there was anything I could do to help. He said, "I don't know. There are so many problems."

"Have you given any thought to what you will do when the fire is finally put out?" I asked.

"No," he said.

"Well, the fire will be out by morning, and I think you had better start planning for what comes next."

"Yes . . . you're right, why don't you put together some suggestions and call back in about an hour," he said.

I agreed, and when I gave him my suggestions, the first suggestion was the formation of an investigating commission to determine the facts. In the interim there was a news report that members of the City Council had met that night, and some of them suggested that the City Council should impanel an investigating committee. The mayor did not respond to my suggestion of an investigating commission. Before noon of the day after the fire, members of the state legislature and of the United States Congress were also suggesting that there should be an official investigation. Reports of the deaths of the women and children sparked demands for grand jury investigations. An independent investigation was an idea whose time had come.

Three days passed. Three days of intense national and international news focused on Philadelphia, the city where police dropped a bomb on a row house whose occupants included women and children—Philadelphia, the first American city to be bombed from the air—Philadelphia, the city where a police bomb started a fire, and the fire department did not fight it.

The mayor, police commissioner and the fire commissioner were interviewed by the network news departments and on the nationally televised morning talk shows. They explained that the bomb was not a bomb, it was an "explosive device." They argued that the MOVE adults could have saved the children by sending them out of the house before the hostilities began, or by surrendering to the police. They said MOVE members were terrorists and Philadelphia was the first American city to be confronted by armed insurgents. Everything they said avoided responsibility and also avoided the nagging question of how a confrontation with a few urban radicals could result in such massive destruction. Nothing which they said ended the inquiries. News reporters began to search for evidence that would fix responsibility. The versions of the tragic events conflicted, and the more they were discussed, the more confused was the view of Philadelphia's government in action.

The explanations did not end the questions because people

everywhere, who believed in the ability of organized society to protect them, wanted to know precisely what went wrong. Four days after our telephone conversation, the mayor called me to say that he was thinking about asking the Chief Justice of the Pennsylvania Supreme Court to impanel an investigating commission. I told him I did not believe a panel appointed by a court would provide the proper context for what had to be done. I said it was his responsibility as mayor to determine what went wrong and that responsibility provided the basis for the appointment of an investigating commission. He said he was concerned that a commission which he appointed might not be viewed as independent and impartial. I said he did not have to claim the commission was independent, but that it was doing the job he could not do because he had to continue to manage the city. He said he would get back to me. A few days later he did get back to me and asked me to recommend the names of persons he could consider for appointment to the commission. I had started thinking about that and sent him my list of names within 24 hours. None of the people I suggested was appointed to the commission.

Information leaks out of the Philadelphia City Hall faster than water leaks out of a sieve, and a few days after I sent my list to the mayor I received telephone calls from various center city aficionados seeking information about the appointment of an investigating commission. The callers discussed rumors about various potential appointees to the commission. I told them I didn't know who the mayor might appoint. I couldn't believe he would appoint some of the persons who were suggested to me. Because the mayor and I had been friends for more than twenty years, some of the callers believed I could influence his decision about the commission. The "political insiders" almost screamed through the telephone, demanding that I advise the mayor against appointing a commission. They wanted him to ride out the storm, to hang tough and wait for the newspapers to become interested in some other story. They were Democrats, and the mayor was the leader of their party. They were afraid that an investigation, which might destroy him politically, might also destroy the party.

The "community activists" who called had been on the cutting edge of efforts to foster social, economic and political changes to help minority communities. Most of them telephoned me because the tragedy cast a pall on their years of work and sacrifice. They believed their work had helped to prepare for the election of Goode as Philadelphia's first black mayor, and they needed assurance that they had not worked in vain. They wanted help understanding the irony that made them feel indirectly accountable for the tragedy. They were also disappointed with themselves. They knew they would have been in the streets demonstrating against the mayor if he were white. They could not bring themselves to denounce what they had worked so hard and so long to accomplish, and they knew they were as unfair as those they worked to replace.

I told everyone who called me it was too soon to make judgments about the tragedy. I explained that the investigation was necessary to determine exactly what was done and by whom. I advised them that the mayor's overall responsibility should not make him liable for everything that happened if there were atrocities which he could not prevent. I asked them to give the investigating commission a fair opportunity to determine the facts.

A few days after he received my recommendations for the commission, the mayor telephoned me to ask if I thought William Brown would make a good chairman of the commission. Bill Brown was an outstanding lawyer. He was a senior partner in the prestigious Philadelphia law firm of Schnader, Harrison, Segal and Lewis. President Nixon had appointed him the first chairman of the United States Equal Employment Opportunity commission. He was the first black person to serve as chairman of a national commission. He and I entered the legal profession in the same year, 1958, and we worked together in 1984 when he was a member of the Pennsylvania Federal Judicial Nominating commission, of which I was chairman. He served on the Philadelphia subcommittee which screened candidates for the position of United States attorney for the Eastern District of Pennsylvania. Our work on that committee resulted in the appointment of Edward Dennis as U.S. Attorney, the first black lawyer to be appointed to that office.

At one critical point in the process, when it appeared that opposition from the Reagan administration would prevent the appointment of any black person, Brown challenged the committee to deliver an ultimatum that Dennis, who was the most qualified candidate, be appointed or the committee would resign in protest. Dennis was appointed. Brown was a Republican, and his selection as chairman of the commission was the clearest signal that the mayor wanted to avoid any charge of a politically biased commission. I told the mayor that I thought Brown would make an excellent chairman, and I also told him I thought a majority of the

members of the commission should be black. I believed that the
trauma which reverberated throughout the city had its greatest
impact on the black community. A black neighborhood was burned
down, and black children and adults were killed. Unhappily, the
ethnic composition of the commission was a consideration. My
generation of Americans lives with the lingering perception of
ethnic distinctions as divisions as well as differences. We have
adjusted to the paradox of demands for racial equality and claims
to a proprietary interest in racial distinctions.

The glorious civil rights movement led us all to a vantage
point where we could see Dr. King's vision of an America freed from
the limitations of racial division, but we had not lived with the
vision long enough to fully absorb its virtues. We were still learning
to have enough trust and goodwill to believe in the vision. It was
hard to suppress old fears.

The mayor invited me to his office to review the names of the
persons he intended to appoint to the commission. It was a
spacious office with paneled walls and deep, soft carpet on the
floor. Behind the mayor's desk there was a huge painting of
snow-capped mountain peaks rising above the clouds. The painting was hung in the place where previous mayors had a painting
of Independence Hall. We sat at a long conference table which was
situated along the wall opposite the desk. When I saw the list, I
realized the mayor was taking a critical political risk. They were
all strong people. They had long- standing reputations for honesty.
They had their own constituencies and positions in the community. Their judgment would be without regard for its impact on the
mayor. He had picked a jury which might condemn him, and I
said, "You may have picked your own hangmen."

"I think they'll be fair," he replied. "All I want is a fair review
of what happened."

My primary criticisms of the mayor's choices for the commission were that there were too many lawyers and that his list did
not include the name of a leader in the business community. I
recommended that he substitute M. Todd Cooke, Vice-Chairman
of the Philadelphia Savings Fund Society, for a judge whose name
was on the list. The mayor agreed to the substitution. The local
news reporters did not have a similar concern for fairness. Their
bent for distortion and innuendo, led them to condemn the
appointment of the commission as soon as the names of the
appointees were announced. They reported very little about the
credentials and community standing of the appointees. Instead

they focused their reports on which of the appointees had contributed money to the mayor's campaign funds in 1983, or had
other relationships with the mayor. Their reports implied that the
appointees were so devoid of character they would ignore the death
and destruction of the tragedy to gain mayor's favor. William
Green, whose law firm had received millions in legal fees while he
was Mayor, and very little from the Goode administration, publicly
criticized the appointment of the commission and the appointees.

The local media worked itself into a frenzy of distortion in an
effort to sink the commission in a sea of distrust before it began
its work. On May 28, 1985, the newly appointed commission
members met for the first time in a conference room at the offices
of Brown's law firm. We knew each other because of previous
relationships or by reputation. I don't believe any of us knew how
much better we would know each other before our work as a
commission was completed.

The Reverend Dr. Audrey Bronson was a former associate
professor of psychology at Cheyney University, a predominantly
black university about forty miles west of the city. She had been a
summa cum laude graduate of Cheyney. She was also the founder
and pastor of the Sanctuary Church of the Open Door. The church
was located in West Philadelphia, not far from the 6200 block of
Osage Avenue. She always held her slender physique erect. There
was a seriousness about her face that announced her superior
intellect. I had not seen her for several years, but I immediately
felt close to her. I knew what she stood for, and I believed we would
work as allies on the commission.

M. Todd Cooke was a graduate of Princeton University and
M.I.T. He was one of a brigade of white business leaders who gave
substance to the civic life of the city. He was reserved and low-key
to the point that his more than six-foot-tall athletic form might be
overlooked in a room with few people. But in a meeting where the
issues were tough and a consensus seemed to be impossible to
find, his insight often made the difference.

I first met Cooke almost twenty years earlier, when he was a
vice-president of another bank, and deeply involved in helping the
city devise financial strategies for financing low-income housing.

Bruce Kauffman was a senior partner in the law firm of
Dilworth, Paxon, Kalish and Kauffman. He was one of
Pennsylvania's leading Republicans, and he had previously served
as a member of the state supreme court. He was a fair jurist and
a very successful lawyer. I had read some of his court opinions,

but beyond that, I knew little about him. I later learned that he was one of the few people I've known whose passion for his position on an issue was equal to my own.

Charisse Lillie, a member of the faculty of Villanova Law School, was a stranger. She was the youngest member of the commission, a generation behind the others. Her bright, dark eyes sparkled with her intelligence, and her round, young face, unadorned by makeup, was so naturally pretty it was stunning. She was one of the few black women who continued to wear their hair in its natural state—very short and very curly. Her genuine, straightforward appearance was an accurate reflection of her mind. Her voice was soft, with a lilt that emphasized the youthfulness of her face.

Father Paul Washington, the Episcopal priest of the Church of the Advocate, located at 18th and Diamond Streets, was the patron saint of the inner city and the eloquent conscience of the dissident and distraught groups which took refuge in his church. He had been a mediator between the police and MOVE members during the 1978 confrontation. He was a black man of medium build, medium complexion and minimal means, like so many thousands of black men who struggled to survive amid the squalor that surrounded the Church of the Advocate. When he spoke he was distinguished from almost all others of any color or conviction. His voice was a deep baritone that should have come from a larger person, and his enunciation was as clear, precise and scholarly as an Oxford professor.

He was a member of the Philadelphia Commission on Human Relations and a member of the anti-establishment who was understood and trusted by the establishment. He had been a hero of the struggles for civil rights, economic opportunity, social justice and political advancement for the disenfranchised whom he loved.

Mrs. Julia M. Chinn was the only representative of the Osage neighborhood on the commission. She lived within a few blocks of the 6200 block of Osage, and she had worked with the residents of that street as President of the Cobbs Creek Town Watch. She recruited them and other residents of the Cobbs Creek area to cooperate in a network of neighbors who tried to protect their homes from crime by their vigilance. Mrs. Chinn was also an officer of the Concerned Block Captains of West Philadelphia. Block captains were elected at community meetings held by the residents of a block. Hundreds of blocks elected captains during the 1960's as part of a Philadelphia More Beautiful program to encourage residents to keep their blocks clean and to decorate them with flowers. Each year prizes were awarded to blocks for exceptional cleanliness and floral displays. Eventually block captains began to assume other leadership roles related to the problems of their streets and their neighbors. Political leaders relied on them as a quick reference into what was happening on a particular street, and city departments began to recognize their influence and to respond to their complaints.

By 1985, the civic and political influence of block captains was established, and they had joined into regional organizations to increase their clout for the betterment of the neighborhoods. Mrs. Chinn was also the only member of the commission who would have to live with the decisions of the commission as part of her daily contact with neighbors who were directly affected by the tragedy.

As Director of Catholic Social Services for the Philadelphia Archdiocese, and a professional social worker, Monsignor Edward P. Cullen had been involved in trying to repair some of the damage left in the wake of the tragedy. Most of the refugees from the fire were temporarily housed and fed at St. Carthage Roman Catholic Church, which was located about three blocks from the 6200 block of Osage. Like Bill Brown and myself, he was born, reared and educated in Philadelphia. Each of us was from the row house neighborhoods that nurtured most of the city's populace. We all had been high school athletes. Brown was an outstanding distance runner; Cullen and I once opposed each other as halfbacks on our respective high school football teams. His quick mind and easy manner made him a delight to talk to, and his capacity for caring for others gave added authority to his views.

Neil J. Welch provided the first half of the prosecutorial experience on the commission. He had been the assistant director of the Philadelphia office of the Federal Bureau of Investigation. In retirement he was a consultant on law enforcement.

Henry S. Ruth, Jr., another lawyer, had served as the third chief prosecutor of the congressional Watergate investigations. He was also Deputy Director of the President's commission on Law Enforcement and Administration of Justice. He was brilliant, and he was the best listener on the commission. When everyone had finished their remarks about a subject, he often helped us understand what we had said and what it all meant. He heard everything: in every nuance and every inflection he heard our true intent despite our words.

He was also deeply involved emotionally with the tragedy. During one discussion of the failure of the fire department to fight the fire, he recalled how he and his family watched the fire growing on their television set until they began to shout in frustration, "Put out the fire . . . put out the fire." His keen sense of decency was outraged by the dimensions of the tragedy, and yet he was equally concerned that every effort was made to protect the rights of those whom we investigated.

I was the only person on the commission whose background included training in explosives, a working relationship with members of MOVE, an executive position with city government, intensive involvement with community organizations, citywide political experience, and a long relationship with the mayor. In September 1952, when I was drafted into the Army, the outcome of the Korean war was still in doubt. I was in basic training when an officer met with me and a group of other trainees who had received high scores in the battery of tests given to new recruits. He offered us the opportunity to volunteer to defuse bombs, locate and dig up land mines, and to otherwise tamper with military high explosives.

I would have laughed at his offer, but he said there were too many bomb disposal experts in Korea and, therefore, those who volunteered would probably be assigned to major airports which accommodated military aircraft. He mentioned cities such as New York, Los Angeles, Chicago and Philadelphia.

He also said that bomb disposal squads only had eight members who only took orders from bomb disposal officers. The dangers inherent in high explosives were modified by the possibility of avoiding Korea and redneck army sergeants.

I was 22 years old and a college graduate. I had not learned how to be afraid of anything, and I wasn't smart enough to consider that an officer in the United States Army would lie. In fact, he didn't lie to everyone. I was one of five black graduates in a class of 25 who graduated from the Explosive Ordinance Disposal School at Aberdeen, Maryland. Twenty of the graduates were assigned to airports at major cities. Five were assigned to combat duty in Korea. If John Africa had met me on the day I learned only the black graduates were sent to Korea, I too might have become a member of MOVE.

In 1967, Mayor James Tate appointed me deputy mayor because he was in a desperate struggle for re-election. Congressman William Barrat was his strongest ally and one of the few

Democratic leaders who had not made a deal with the Republican candidate who was ahead of Tate in all of the political polls. In June the incumbent police commissioner resigned, and Barrat insisted that Tate appoint Deputy police commissioner Frank Rizzo as the new police commissioner. Rizzo had worked his way up from the ranks of patrolmen and had a reputation for using excessive force in making arrests. That reputation was strongest in Philadelphia's vast black community, where Tate needed to win an overwhelming majority of the votes.

My appointment as the first black deputy mayor was intended to offset Rizzo's appointment as police commissioner. To make the point clear, Tate announced that I would supervise policy for the police department. That role afforded me an opportunity to learn about police training, tactics and equipment.

My relationship with the MOVE organization began with a visit from a tall, pleasant young man, who introduced himself as Bob Africa, and his husky companion, who said his name was Gerald Africa. It was 1971, and I was Executive Director of the Philadelphia Urban Coalition, a local duplication of the National Urban Coalition, which advocated improvement of the quality of life in the inner city and was funded by Philadelphia's major corporations.

It was my job to work with, and provide funds to, inner city community groups and some of the most alienated groups in the city. We funded programs as disparate as a baseball team in a predominantly Polish neighborhood and the breakfast program of the Black Panther Party. I hadn't talked to Bob and Gerald Africa very long when I realized that MOVE was the most alienated group I had ever encountered. There was an incident when I was an invited guest at a Black Muslim convocation in Philadelphia which demonstrated the extent of MOVE's alienation. Several members of MOVE who were in the audience disrupted the proceedings by shouting objections to the racial exclusivity of the Black Muslims. This was at a time in the 1970's when the Muslims were at the height of their power in Philadelphia, and no one challenged them. If the leader of the convocation had not given an order to avoid hurting the MOVE members, I was certain they would be severely beaten by the Muslim guards who surrounded them.

Disrupting meetings was one of the tactics MOVE members used for spreading their message. They often spent hours explaining the teachings of John Africa to me, and I understood their message. They were profane and provocative, but they were not violent or dangerous in those days. Their public provocations and profanity made them targets of police harassment and abuse. In 1974, I wrote a column for the Sunday Philadelphia Inquirer in which I defended MOVE's right to freedom from police abuse.

As I thought about my appointment to the investigating commission, I wondered if it was more than coincidence which afforded me the experiences that prepared me for that critical moment in the history of the city. I also wondered if I would be able to do anything that might help to atone for the deaths of the children who, unlike the adults who were killed, were not given the chance to choose between life without John Africa or death with him.

The newly appointed commission members sat around a large, octagonal conference table which almost filled the room on the thirty-sixth floor of the office building at 16th and Market Streets. The building was a gleaming tower of glass and steel starkly contrasted to the gray granite walls of City Hall two blocks away. The elevators rose quickly and silently to the elegantly furnished suite which housed part of Bill Brown's law firm.

Each commission member received a personal telephone call from the mayor requesting their service on the commission, but the letters of appointment were not addressed to them individually. The letters were addressed to Brown as chairman and to "Members of the Osage Avenue commission." The letters expressed the mayor's appreciation to the appointees as a group for agreeing to serve on the commission, but they did not appoint them, nor did they indicate by what power or authority the mayor appointed them. The shortcomings of the letters were an immediate concern of the commission members.

Henry Ruth was first to mention the inadequacies of the letters and to suggest that the commission make certain it was legally organized. The members faced a thicket of legal problems which would be exacerbated if they were not legally authorized to investigate the tragedy. The Fraternal Order of Police certainly would file a lawsuit to challenge the legality of the commission. Decisions and recommendations of the commission might adversely affect the careers and legal status of everyone involved in the events of May 13, and therefore the establishment of the legal authority of the commission was essential.

I suggested that rather than request new appointment letters from the mayor, we obtain an executive order establishing the commission, outlining its objectives and responsibilities, naming its members and authorizing it to subpoena witnesses and documents. Brown assigned me the task of writing a proposed executive order which could be submitted to the mayor and the city solicitor.

The members did not like the mayor's designation of the commission as the "Osage Avenue commission." They thought the name did not fully describe their purpose. Some of the members suggested "The MOVE commission," but I objected to that name because it suggested that our purpose was limited to an investigation of the MOVE organization. Neil Welch suggested "The Philadelphia Special Investigation commission," and there was immediate agreement on that name.

The credibility of the commission and the scope of the investigation evolved as the central issues of the first meeting. Accusations by the press, by former Mayor Green and by the chairman of the local Republican Party that the commission members could not be impartial because they were appointed by the mayor troubled some of the members. The first discussion of trying to reassure the press ended when I said that no matter what the other members did, I would not respond to a suggestion that I was so devoid of character I would ignore the deaths of children to curry favor with the mayor.

Discussion of the scope of the investigation quickly centered on appropriate limits on the inquiry. The most pressing question was how the commission should handle evidence of criminal conduct. The prevailing view was that the commission should only report facts without making judgments about the legal effect of the facts. I argued that if we found facts which clearly indicated there was criminal conduct, we should refer that information to the appropriate legal authorities.

The first meeting was an accurate indication of the discussions and debates that would follow throughout the life of the commission. There was an unexpressed understanding that we were a jury who would render a verdict on more than the tragic events of May 13. Our determinations would affect the lives and careers of every participant. We knew that we might become the instrument for removing the mayor from office, or for so badly damaging his record that he could not be re-elected to office. We knew that we would render a profound pronouncement on the effectiveness of Philadelphia's government and the humaneness of its community. While we did not know what we would learn from the investigation, we knew it would not be praiseworthy. The death and destruction we were charged to investigate were symptoms of a serious malady. Whether our exploratory operation on the city administration would uncover a terminal cancer of brutal criminality or a benign polyp of inexcusable ineptness and negligence we did not know.

We had to probe with enough skill to avoid inflicting additional damage while we tried to pinpoint the source of the ailment. As the first meeting ended, I raised the issue which had been avoided. It was too obvious an issue to have been forgotten, but it was a consideration which added a dimension to the tragedy no one wanted to confront. "There is a large segment of the black community who will expect us to determine if race was a factor in what happened," I said. "I believe there are many black people who believe this death and destruction would not have happened in a white neighborhood."

The silence in the room was a poignant response. Brown ended the silence when he said, "I think you're right. That is certainly something we will have to look at."

Two days after the first meeting I sent Brown a proposed executive order establishing the Philadelphia Special Investigation commission. The proposed executive order cited the sections of the city's charter which authorized the creation of the commission, listed the names of the members of the commission, established the term of the existence of the commission, provided for a budget and a final report, and granted subpoena power to the commission. On June 4, 1985 the mayor issued executive order No. 4-85. The order did not establish the commission, nor did it name it the Philadelphia Special Investigation commission. The order failed to appoint the members of the commission, or to establish a budget or a term of service.

The first working meeting of the commission began at 7:30 A.M. on Saturday, June 8, 1985. We met in a larger conference room with a long, rectangular table and a smaller side table where there were breakfast pastries, fruits and coffee. The mayor's June 4 executive order was reviewed and rejected. It was difficult to understand why the mayor and the city solicitor had failed to appoint the commission and name its members in the order, as well as include the other provisions of the proposed order. The necessity of the specifics was so obvious that the members of the commission began to suspect the mayor's motives in omitting them.

Brown told the members he was certain the mayor would amend the order to include the language we wanted, but he could not allay suspicions, and there was a consensus that the commission should submit to the mayor the executive order it wanted, and if he refused to issue it the members of the commission would resign. The members agreed with the provisions in the proposed order, but Ruth and Brown objected to certain language that established the commission as existing within the Law Department of the city. I had followed the specific authorization for investigative committees in the city charter, which only provided for them within the Law Department.

Brown and Ruth argued that the commission should be directly authorized by the mayor, based on his broad executive powers. The commission agreed to submit another proposed executive order to the mayor which was based on his executive powers and which included the provisions of the first proposed order which established the commission, named its members, provided for its funding and set forth the parameters of its authority to investigate the events of May 13. Brown was directed by the commission to present the new proposed order to the mayor and to tell him that without it the members of the commission could not serve. On June 19, the mayor issued the second proposed order as executive order No. 5-85, and rescinded the previous order.

The development of the order authorizing the commission was a critical point in the relationship between the commission, the mayor and his administration. The commission established an arm's-length relationship with the mayor and determined that it would be the master of the terms under which it would work. Commission members were not certain the mayor would accede to their demand for their version of an executive order, but when they voted for their version it was with steel-edged determination. There was a feeling in the room that they would start their work on the right foot, or they would not start at all.

I was certain the mayor would grant them almost anything they wanted because he had no other option. I was also certain that most of the members of the commission voted to demand their version of an executive order because they wanted to send the mayor a message. It was a clear and concise message which said, "We are calling the shots."

9

THE SEARCH
FOR FACTS

Once its authority was established, the commission began the work of organizing a staff and planning the investigation. The meetings were long. Details were thoroughly examined and discussed. We knew the success of our work depended on our diligence. One of the first issues which tested the philosophical mettle of the commissioners was whether former members of the Philadelphia Police and Fire Departments could be hired as investigators on the commission's staff. The commission had, by vote, authorized hiring Carl Singley, who was Dean of Temple University Law School, as special counsel to the commission, and William Lytton, former Deputy U.S. Attorney for the Eastern District of Pennsylvania, as staff director and counsel. Brown was then authorized to hire whatever additional staff was necessary, except that former members of the Philadelphia Police and Fire Departments could not be hired.

Reverend Bronson and I were absent from the commission meeting on June 22, when it was decided that former Philadelphia police and firefighters should not be hired as staff investigators, but that someone with prior ties to those departments could be hired as a consultant. By the July 1 meeting, Brown had hired Lytton; Singley; Emerson D. Moran, as communications officer; Neil P. Shanahan, former FBI special agent, as chief investigator; and Maryia O'Connor, as secretary to the commission. At the meeting Lytton reported that it was difficult to find black investigators who had retired or resigned from the FBI or other federal agencies. I objected to the decision of the previous meeting which excluded former Philadelphia police and firefighters from employment on the commission's staff.

It was my position that the commission's impartiality should begin with selecting its staff, and individuals should be considered for the staff positions based on their merits. I opposed any discrimination based on former employment with the city. Kaufff-man disagreed. He was concerned about the affect on the public's perception of the investigation if former Philadelphia employees were involved. He argued that one of the important issues to be investigated was whether MOVE members tried to surrender and were shot by police. He did not believe a former Philadelphia officer should investigate those facts. Cooke agreed with Kauffman. Shanahan explained that if he was prohibited from hiring former Philadelphia police and firefighters, a very large pool of qualified people would be eliminated, and the opportunities to hire black investigators would be diminished.

I looked across the highly polished table and briefly made eye contact with Kauffman. I wanted him to see my determination to avoid any form of discrimination in selecting investigators and to make certain there was every possible opportunity to hire qualified black investigators. The worst result would have been sending an all-white team of investigators into a black neighborhood to in-vestigate the tragedy.

Father Washington also turned toward Kauffman and said that past practices of racial discrimination in federal agencies had reduced the number of black investigators who were former employees of those agencies, and we would validate that past discrimination if we now eliminated former city employees. He said that our only standards should be integrity and competence. Kauffman did not relent in his opposition to former city police and firefighters, and I wondered if he understood that the discussion was moving swiftly toward a racial division of the commission members. Reverend Bronson pushed the discussion closer to the brink of a racial split when she said the commission would seek serious trouble if it gave the appearance of racial discrimination in selecting investigators.

Once more I looked into Kauffman's eyes. He stared back at me and lifted his square chin. I knew he wasn't ready to relent. Charisse Lillie raised a question about the effectiveness of in-vestigators who were formerly city employees. Kauffman used her question to try to bridge the issue of hiring black investigators. He said that it was important for the commission to have racial balance on its staff, but former city police officers and firefighters were members of the Fraternal Order of Police; the Guardian Civic League, an organization of black police officers; and the Fire-fighters Association, and each of those groups had endorsed the actions of the police and firefighters on May 13.

Monsignor Cullen spoke softly, almost nonchalantly, and said that if it was necessary to insure that there were black investigators on the staff he would, understand hiring former city employees. What he did not say, to complete his position, was, "and the public would certainly understand that." Kauffman shifted his position slightly after Monsignor Cullen spoke. Kauffman said that if the commission had to hire investigators who were former city employees, it should first search for investigators from every other available source to be certain that former city employees were all there was. Kauffman suggested trying former members of the state police. Brown reminded Kauffman that a state police helicopter delivered the bomb to the roof of the MOVE house, and that the agency's past record on hiring minorities was not good.

I tried to broaden the issue beyond racial considerations and said that discriminating against former city employees would not only effect black former employees. I thought the commission should be completely impartial and should not indulge in any form of discrimination. Now everyone looked at Kauffman. The weight of the arguments was clearly against his position. It was time for him to concede, but he lifted his chin a little higher, in a gesture that would be repeated throughout all of the commission's debates, as he made his final argument. He said that every police officer who took part in the May 13 incident was afraid of being made a scapegoat by the investigation. He thought time was of the essence in order to win public confidence and avoid any appearance of impropriety, and therefore the commission should avoid hiring former city employees.

His argument that police officers were afraid of being made scapegoats did not jibe with his conclusion unless his implication was that white police officers who took part in the May 13 operation might fear that black investigators would not treat them fairly. Reverend Bronson sat on the same side of the table as Kauffman, and she had to lean forward to look at him as she spoke. Her voice was sharp, and her words were quick and decisive. She used Kauffman's terms to bring the debate to a conclusion. "What is weightier," she asked, "racial balance or the public's percep-tion?" Kauffman did not answer her. Her question ended the debate.

By mid-July six investigators had been hired. They had a total of 153 years of experience in law enforcement and investigations. They were recruited from Illinois, Connecticut, Virginia, Maryland and Pennsylvania. One of them started his career as a Philadelphia policeman, but he had worked for twenty years as a special agent of the U.S. Treasury's Alcohol, Tobacco and Firearms Criminal Enforcement Division after leaving the Philadelphia Police Department. Four of the investigators were black. All of them had extensive education and training in investigation, and they had all received various special commendations and awards for outstanding performance. Their work demonstrated that they were the best six investigators to search for the facts of what happened on May 13.

In addition to the investigative staff and the commission's own team of forensic pathologists, 45 law students volunteered to work for the commission. Philadelphia law firms assigned eleven of their summer associates to work full time for the commission. Various civic organizations and scores of individuals offered the commission their help and suggested areas which needed to be investigated. There was substantial evidence that the news media's strident efforts to discredit the commission had failed. The Philadelphia community joined in the search for facts that might answer the questions which troubled everyone.

The plan for the investigation was simple—review everything, inquire into everything and interview everyone who had any information about the tragedy. The commission demanded that city officials and departments provide them with copies of every document related to MOVE or to the complaints and controversy on Osage Avenue. Subpoenas were sent to officials demanding reports, memoranda, personal notes, minutes of meetings and any other writing, or audio or video tapes. Documents were delivered to the commission's offices. They described the years of the city's tormented relationship with MOVE. The Department of Licenses and Inspections had not been permitted to inspect the MOVE house on Osage Avenue. The inspectors were threatened with violence by MOVE members, and the police department would not respond to the inspectors' request for assistance. When employees of the water department attempted to turn off water service to the MOVE house because water and sewer bills had not been paid, they were also threatened with violence, and the police department also ignored their requests for assistance.

Community relations employees met with the Osage Avenue

residents and dutifully reported their complaints and their growing frustration with the situation created by the MOVE house. They reported the fortification of the house. They warned that a violent confrontation was inevitable. Their reports were filed away by their superiors. Prior to May 13, 1985, there were thousands of pages of critical information within the city bureaucracy which together sounded an alarm about the danger on Osage Avenue. Some of the information was circulated upward to middle management workers who decided their superiors would be annoyed by the warnings, and so they filed the warnings out of sight. MOVE was a troublesome problem no one wanted to confront, and none of the middle level bureaucrats wanted to raise the issue.

The police department was not forthcoming in releasing reports and other documents. They stalled for a time. They tried to limit the extent of the commission's demands for documents. They were no match for Lytton and Brown, who were relentless in seeking every scrap of documentation that existed. In the end the police department surrendered every document.

The search for documentation resulted in responses from 36 city departments and agencies that were computer-coded into 566 evidence categories. Hundreds of still photographs and several video tapes were also obtained and catalogued.

Investigators and volunteers went into the Osage Avenue neighborhood and knocked on doors, soliciting interviews from residents who might have witnessed the events of May 13. They also conducted more than a thousand interviews, some lasting four or five hours, with police officers, firefighters, officials, neighborhood residents and others who had information about the tragedy. One of the targets of the investigation was discovering exactly what explosives were used to make the bomb. That meant interviewing the members of the police Bomb Disposal Unit. Lt. Frank Powell was commander of the Bomb Disposal Unit, and the other members were Daniel Angelucci, John Biggins, Thomas Boyce, William Klien and James Laarkamp.

Powell, Klein and Laarkamp were interviewed; however, after an FBI agent admitted he had made false statements to his superiors and to the commission about the amount of C-4 military explosive he gave to the Philadelphia police (he gave them at least 38 pounds of the powerful explosive), the members of the Bomb Disposal Unit decided to refuse to testify to avoid self-incrimination.

Asserting the protection of the Fifth Amendment, after the truth was revealed about how much military explosive had been given to them, reflected on their intent in using the powerful explosive. Police officers are trained to know the elements of various crimes, and are presumed to know when conduct may be criminal. Therefore, when a police officer asserts his right to refuse to testify because he may provide evidence that could implicate him in a crime, it is fair to assume he knows the legal effect of what he has done.

The constitutional rights, employment rights and personal rights of individual police officers were one of the earliest concerns of the commission. Police officers, who were not responsible for the decisions which required their participation in the tragedy, would be primary witnesses during the public hearings. Their prominence as witnesses might create the impression that they were primarily responsible for the death and destruction. Consideration of their rights, as well as the rights of other witnesses, began when the commission developed its rules of procedure for the public hearings. The first issues were whether witnesses would be permitted to make opening statements, cross-examine other witnesses and respond to unfavorable testimony about their conduct. The commission quickly agreed that the hearings were not adversary proceedings, and therefore cross-examination of witnesses would not be allowed. Every witness would be first examined by Lytton, or his deputy, Graham McDonald, and then each commissioner could question the witness.

The commission also decided very quickly that any witness who believed he was the victim of unfair, inaccurate or unfavorable testimony could file an affidavit in response to that testimony, which would become part of the official record. The right of a witness to make an opening statement was a more difficult problem. Brown opposed allowing opening statements because he thought they might interject irrelevant matters and delay the proceedings. Ruth and Kauffman agreed with Brown, and the other members of the commission agreed that it was important to expedite the public hearings, and therefore opening statements should not be allowed.

I dissented from the consensus. Although the witnesses did not have a legal or constitutional right to make an opening statement, they would be in a glaring spotlight of public opinion. For many of the police officers, their testimony would be the first and only time in their lives they would appear on television. Their families and friends would be affected by the perceptions and opinions which resulted from their testimony. There was no certainty that the questions asked by the commission would provide the witnesses with an opportunity to express their personal views of what they did and why they did it. Denying them an opening statement was unfair.

Monsignor Cullen was the first commission member to agree with me. Expediency was not a sufficient reason to deny witnesses any opportunity to represent themselves and their actions, and the affidavits allowed by the rules would not receive the public exposure of testimony on television. Brown argued that the witnesses were not on trial, nor were they accused of anything; therefore there was no need for them to defend conduct. Ruth agreed with Brown again. He thought that it was paramount to preserve the fact-finding function of the commission and that allowing opening statements might suggest that the commission was passing judgment on the witnesses. The legal niceties of the hearings would not affect the television audience. They would make judgments about individual witnesses. Their opinions could be just as detrimental to the careers and lives of the witnesses as any action by the commission. I reminded the other commissioners that the neighbors and fellow workers of the witnesses would see and hear the testimony. News commentators would interpret the testimony, and their families would share whatever public opinion resulted from their testimony.

Every person who played any role in the tragedy had to have some personal reaction to it. An opening statement might be the only opportunity to express personal feelings about what happened. Father Washington and Reverend Bronson agreed that some opening statement should be allowed as a matter of fairness. The opinion of the commission shifted, and it decided to allow each witness the right to make an opening statement not to exceed five minutes.

The Fifth Amendment rights of the witnesses presented the commission with legal problems. Mayor Goode promised to dismiss any city employee who did not fully cooperate with the commission's investigation. The Philadelphia Home Rule Charter provided for the dismissal of a city employee who asserted his constitutional rights against self-incrimination in connection with his public duties.

Even though members of the Bomb Disposal Unit gave statements to the commission's investigators, their lawyers advised the commission that they would plead the Fifth Amendment if they were called to testify at the televised hearings. It was the middle of October, and the public hearings had begun. The commission had successfully resisted efforts by F.O.P. lawyers to have the hearings enjoined as illegal. Early polls indicated that the televised hearings were viewed by at least 250,000 households. The public television station which broadcast the hearings enjoyed its best ratings ever. The skeptics had been silenced, but the effectiveness of the investigation would be determined, in part, by the commission's ability to establish the facts surrounding the manufacture of the bomb.

The bomb was the dramatic core of the tragedy. Although it was not the decisive element of causation for the death and destruction, it was the focus of public attention. The bomb had to be explained and understood. Every fact about its existence had to be explored. An intense debate was initiated when lawyers representing members of the Bomb Disposal Unit said they would plead the Fifth Amendment if they were summoned to testify. Kauffman, Brown and I argued that the commission should insist that the mayor keep his promise to dismiss any city employee who did not fully cooperate with the investigation. Ruth countered that no one should suffer a penalty for asserting rights guaranteed by the Constitution. The right against self-incrimination was not limited because a public employee was dismissed for asserting that right. Court decisions upheld the charter provision authorizing the dismissal of employees who took the Fifth Amendment.

Lytton told the commission he believed some of the Bomb Disposal Unit members were advised by their lawyers to take the Fifth because they might give evidence that would incriminate other police officers. That was not a valid reason for pleading the Fifth. Kauffman submitted a memorandum of law to the commission which outlined the legal basis for overcoming the Fifth Amendment and explained the procedure for submitting the recalcitrant witness to a court proceeding where a judge would hear the testimony in secret and then decide if the witness had valid grounds for asserting the Fifth Amendment. The debate went on during luncheon breaks from the hearings, and in the evenings at the conclusion of the hearings. The commissioners wanted to protect constitutional rights. Most of their backgrounds had caused them to understand the necessity of protecting individual rights in the face of majority opposition to those rights, but the validity of the investigation was at stake. They had to develop the facts about the bomb.

Kauffman and I were adamant in the position that the Bomb

Disposal Unit should not avoid public scrutiny. We convinced the commission that the members of the Bomb Disposal Unit should be called to testify and required to plead the Fifth Amendment repeatedly in response to specific questions about their conduct. Brown concurred with our position and said that fairness to the police officers who agreed to testify required us to expose the Bomb Disposal Unit members to the same public opinion the other officers faced.

On October 23, after they were notified that the Bomb Disposal Unit would be required to appear before the commission to plead the Fifth Amendment, F.O.P. lawyers filed a motion in Federal District Court to enjoin the commission from requiring the officers to plead the Fifth Amendment before television cameras. Judge James McGirr Kelly agreed with the F.O.P. lawyers and issued an order prohibiting the commission from requiring a witness to testify in public when the commission had been notified that the witness intended to plead the Fifth Amendment. The judge did permit the commission to announce publicly that a witness was summoned but would not be required to testify publicly because that witness had stated an intention to plead the Fifth.

As soon as Judge Kelly issued the order, the F.O.P. lawyers had letters hand-delivered to the commission, notifying it that the members of the Bomb Disposal Unit would plead the Fifth, but that they were willing to meet with the commission in an executive session. Judge Kelly's order was a setback to the inquiry into the bomb and other explosives used on May 13, but the commission had another option. The commission decided to call its investigators as witnesses to read into the public record the statements which Bomb Disposal Unit members gave during their interviews.

When the F.O.P. lawyers learned of the commission's decision, they telephoned Judge Kelly's chambers and requested a further hearing for the morning of October 24 to seek an order prohibiting the interview statements. The short, unimposing physique of the judge was impressive in his flowing black robe as he looked down from the thronelike judicial seat that dominated each of the District Court courtrooms. Before him were the same lawyers he had listened to the day before when he issued the order protecting witnesses from pleading their Fifth Amendment rights in public: Robert Mozenter, the short, pudgy and pugnacious chief counsel of the F.O.P.; Dean Carl Singley, a slender black man who always spoke as though he were delivering a major lecture at the law school; and Ralph Teti, an assistant city solicitor who was present only because the city was required to be represented.

Judge Kelly was a new judge. His legal career had been focused on public utilities law and representation of the Philadelphia Republican Party. It was the type of experience that made him an expert negotiator and compromiser. His first order was the best compromise he could fashion. The police would not be required to plead the Fifth on television, but the commission could publicly announce that they had asserted their Fifth Amendment rights. Kelly listened patiently as Mozenter complained that the commission intended to have investigators testify from their notes of what was said to them by Bomb Disposal Unit members. When Mozenter's argument became repetitious, Kelly interrupted him to ask why a person who heard the statement of another person could not testify under oath as to what he heard?

Mozenter replied that the statements were forced from the officers because of the threat to their employment, and that the commission was using a "backdoor" tactic to negate the judge's order. Mozenter also complained that as attorney for the police, he was not permitted to cross-examine the witnesses about the accuracy of their notes. When Kelly had heard all that Mozenter had to say, he again explained the purpose of his previous order which was to try to balance the equities between the legitimate investigatory pursuits of the commission and the constitutional rights of the Bomb Disposal Unit members. He refuted Mozenter's arguments when he said, "A police officer or any other witness has a right to assert the Fifth Amendment, but that does not mean that if that officer at some other time made a statement or did something in the presence of another person, that person cannot come forward and under oath so testify."

By 9:30 A.M., the hearing was over. Judge Kelly dealt the final crushing blow to the legal obstacles to the investigation. As the lawyers left his courtroom it was clear that the commission had overcome the last major hurdle to presenting the evidence concerning the bomb. The judge's decision also made it clear that the court would not attempt to supervise the investigation. That was the important result. In addition to building the bomb, which was an improvisation attempted to save a failed operation, the Bomb Disposal Unit played a central role in the tactical plans for May 13. The investigation into the organization of the police department discovered that the tactical plans were developed by two members of the Firearms Training and Range Unit which was within the

Training Bureau, and the Bomb Disposal Unit was also within the Training Bureau. Police Commissioner Sambor was chief inspector of the Training Bureau just prior to his appointment as police commissioner.

There was no strategic or administrative reason for assigning the tactical planning to the Training Bureau, and the investigation by Neil P. Shanahan, the commission's chief investigator, uncovered eleven critical errors in the tactical plan. They were:

Failure to devote enough time to planning;
Relying on a previous plan that was known by MOVE;
Failure to develop alternate plans;
Beginning the plan with an ultimatum;
Permitting MOVE to dictate the conditions;
Using untried tactics such as high explosives;
Inadequate communication and coordination;
A lack of adequate intelligence information;
Failure to utilize available experience;
Failure to exercise command and control;
Failure to critique the tactics before May 13.

In his investigatory report on the department, Shanahan wrote of the Bomb Disposal Unit, "To say the Bomb Disposal Unit was out of control is an understatement. They had little or no leadership or oversight . . . "

Many of the ultimate failures of the police were the result of inadequacies in initial recruitment and training. As to recruitment, Shanahan reported, "Unfortunately their entry level standards stink. You do not have to be a high school graduate to apply for a job in the police department. Their test standards are not known except to say that if you pass they consider you a high school graduate equivalent."

In assessing the department's sensitivity to the racial dimensions of the tragedy and of urban law enforcement, Shanahan reviewed the department's minority hiring policies and concluded, "They have never made any progress except that which was required of them by the courts. Not one step has ever been done voluntarily that I know of. Once again, attitudes have not changed at all." Shanahan reported that the general attitude among Philadelphia's police was to be "proud for all the wrong reasons. It is characterized by a feeling that nobody can tell us how to do our job. We certainly do not need any civilian review. It's 'us against them.' They consistently exhibit a virtual disregard for and lack of compliance with Supreme Court decisions regarding the Fourth, Fifth and Sixth Amendments to the Constitution, and as such are constantly in a position to pay the price for this attitude. A classic example of their attitude problem was their reaction to this commission's investigation, ranging anywhere from benign resistance to outright stonewalling. The ease with which they could lie under oath was astonishing, even to the most committed cynic."

The analysis of the police department was critical to the investigation because the attitudes, departmental relationships and ability of police personnel determined how they responded to direction from the civilian leadership of the city, and how they defined the parameters of their powers as police officers. Police operations within densely populated urban neighborhoods must be precise. When those operations involve high-powered automatic weapons and high explosives, their precision must be almost perfect. That requires highly disciplined, highly motivated and carefully controlled police personnel. These were life-and-death requirements the moment Sambor and the other leaders considered making the bomb. The bomb that was made reflected the failures in the police structure. Shanahan reported that Bomb Disposal Unit members believed their expertise was greater than it was, and no one in the police department knew the limits on that expertise. He further reported he could not find any command officer who had any control or oversight over the Bomb Disposal Unit.

He reported that the unit's members were not accountable for their inventory of high explosives, and they suffered individual impairments which should have precluded them from managing explosives. One of them had a severe nervous disability. Another suffered from a back disorder that required high to heavy doses of prescription drugs daily. Still another suffered from narcolepsy. The Bomb Disposal Unit might be best evaluated by information the investigation uncovered concerning one of the unit's tests of explosives. The unit was testing homemade breaching devices, designed to blow holes in walls, when one of the unit's members stood under the test platform during the explosion to see if the blast would harm him. When the members of the unit were questioned about that incident, none of them thought it was odd.

Most of the May 13 operation was assigned to the police Stakeout Unit. The Stakeout Unit was in the Tactical Division of

the special Patrol Bureau. Each of the four firing positions established in houses on Osage Avenue and Pine Street was manned
by members of the Stakeout Unit. They were armed with automatic
weapons, including a .50-caliber machine gun. They were the ones
who were in the best positions to observe what happened. They
were the shooters on May 13.

Most Stakeout Unit members had more than ten years
experience as police officers. They were touted as an elite critical
action unit. At one point during the commission's discussions of
the information obtained by investigators, commissioner Welch
recalled his experience with the Stakeout Unit during his tenure
in the Philadelphia office of the FBI. He said that they were officers
who shot first and asked questions later. Membership in the
Stakeout Unit was akin to admittance into a brotherhood of
hazardous duty police. They set ambushes for the most dangerous
felons—armed robbers and murderers. They led the charges into
barricaded situations. They were committed to daily action based
on the combat premise of "kill or be killed."

The commission's investigators planned to interview at least
two hundred of the five hundred police officers who were involved
in the May 13 operation, including all of the Bomb Disposal Unit
and Stakeout Unit officers. Before they began their interviews, they
reviewed reports of the police department's investigation of the
tragedy. The reports included interviews of some of the same
officers the commission wanted to interview. The police department interviewers only asked each officer his name, rank and
badge number and whether or not he fired his weapon. No
information was gathered about what the officers saw, heard or
did on May 13. The only conclusion to be reached from the police
department investigation was that it was purposefully superficial.
The investigators asked enough questions to claim they had
investigated the facts, but not enough to uncover information
which might fix responsibility for various actions.

After reviewing the police investigation, the commission's
investigators decided they would use the narrative form of interview which provided the best opportunities for the interviewees to
volunteer information. Each police officer who was interviewed
was accompanied by a lawyer provided by the F.O.P. As the
investigators questioned the police they learned that some of them
relied on their lawyer for direction on answering questions, while
others did not appear to want to be represented by a lawyer. There
were occasions when officers contacted the investigators without

their lawyers present to indicate that they wanted to provide additional information to the commission, but the lawyers were preventing them to protect other police officers. Some of the interviews lasted for hours because the lawyers continually interrupted the questioning to caucus with the officer being questioned.

Each interview was reduced to writing on a form which the commission called a "302." The officers were not asked to sign the 302, and copies of the 302 were not given to the officer or his lawyer. The 302's were the notes of the interview as recorded by the interviewing investigators. They provided the basis for deciding which officers would be required to testify at the public hearings, and they were the base of information which Lytton and the commissioners used to help develop their questions. They also became the battleground on which the F.O.P. lawyers waged a battle of acrimony and accusation against the fairness of the commission during the hearings. Brown and other commission members were angered by the tactics of the F.O.P. lawyers. On more than one occasion Brown and Lytton complained bitterly about the conduct of the F.O.P. lawyers during the interviews and on every other occasion when they interacted with the commission.

I tried unsuccessfully to allay the anger expressed by Brown and Lytton by suggesting that the F.O.P lawyers knew they were fighting against the tide of public opinion and legal precedent, and so they were forced to use desperate tactics. It was my opinion that the commission should not take them seriously and should try to avoid the verbal confrontations the lawyers were constantly trying to initiate.

The lawyers were trying to provoke some legal error or public relations mistake that might provide them with grounds for enjoining the investigation or at least discrediting it. Their tactics did delay the investigation and made the commission's tasks more difficult. Their tactics and their demeanor were always at least exasperating and at most personally offensive.

Brown and Lytton used words like "obnoxious" and "unprofessional" in describing the F.O.P. lawyers. At one point, as we approached the beginning of the hearings, I was certain there was enough animosity between Brown, the commission's staff and the F.O.P. lawyers to reduce the hearings to a shouting match, and maybe even a physical altercation. When Brown spoke of the lawyers there was something in his eyes that reflected the toughness that was a part of his personality long before he became a successful lawyer. It was what I had seen in the faces of my friends and enemies on the streets where I grew up. It was reassuring to know that Brown was still in touch with the values which spawned him. I was certain that whatever tactics the lawyers tried at the hearings, they would not be a match for Brown.

There were also difficulties in arranging interviews with the boy, Birdie Africa, and Ramona Africa. The commission needed to interview Ramona, who was the only surviving adult from the MOVE house. She was under arrest and charged with various crimes. The criminal charges against her made it unlikely that she would make any statements to the commission, since those statements could be used against her by the prosecutors. Still the commission had to try to interview her. One of the precepts of the MOVE organization was that they always represented themselves in legal proceedings. Through years of tumultuous courtroom appearances the legal system had adapted to MOVE, and judges assigned lawyers to assist MOVE members. One possible channel to Ramona was through the lawyer assigned to assist her. Another was through Gerald Africa, MOVE's Minister of Information.

Father Washington agreed to use his contacts to try to reach Ramona and ask her to grant the commission an interview, and I agreed to talk to Gerald. When I reached him by telephone, he said he was genuinely pleased to hear from me and that he hoped I would make certain the commission conducted a thorough investigation and named the persons who "murdered" the MOVE members. I assured him that he could trust all of the members of the commission and told him he could help our investigation by agreeing to an interview and by asking Ramona to agree to one as well. He did not respond. I knew the pause meant he was gathering his thoughts for a "MOVE tirade." Sooner or later in every conversation with a member of MOVE, a tirade based on the truth as enunciated by John Africa and focused on whatever complaint troubled MOVE, was inevitable. There was a certain cadence and profanity that marked the tirades, as if they had been rehearsed. It was like pushing a button and the same, sudden rush of words poured from MOVE members as if they shared a common brain.

Experience had taught me there was no point in trying to interrupt Gerald. He condemned the evils of the "system." He railed against the injustice that resulted in his MOVE brothers and sisters being convicted and sentenced to prison for killing a police officer in 1978, and he almost screamed that the fire could not have killed John Africa. Then, suddenly, he was calm, and he said, "None of this had to happen. We wanted to negotiate with the mayor. In March we sent him word that we wanted to negotiate, but we never heard from him."

"What was there to negotiate?" I asked. "You wanted your people released from prison, and the mayor didn't have the power to release them."

"It wasn't like that. We knew he couldn't release them, but he could use his influence to get a review of the court record. We knew that if we got a fair review of the court record, we could demonstrate that there was no evidence to show that anyone from MOVE killed that cop. We sent word that we wanted you to be one of the negotiators to review the record, and when we did that we didn't hear anymore."

"Why didn't you contact me?" I asked.

"It was no use if the mayor wasn't going to negotiate," he said.

"That doesn't make sense," I said. "Why would the mayor object to me?"

"It must have been a political thing."

"There was no reason."

"There must have been . . . he wouldn't do it."

I told Gerald that whatever had happened to their efforts to negotiate, that should not prevent them from cooperating with the only opportunity they would have to determine what happened on May 13 and who was responsible for the deaths of the MOVE members.

"I may talk to your commission, but Ramona can't. The organization has decided that she must not talk to your commission."

"She'll talk to us if you ask her," I said. "As far as I can tell there is not much left of your organization."

"You don't know about our organization. We're still strong, and we have decided that Ramona must not talk to your commission."

I argued with him for more than an hour. I tried to convince him that the commission's investigation was MOVE's best chance to learn the truth about what happened. He ended our conversation with another "MOVE tirade." He knew the truth about May 13. The truth was that the system decided to destroy MOVE once and for all, and it used its puppet mayor to do it. He said that the people would understand that the system was afraid of MOVE, and that would make MOVE stronger.

When I reported to the commission that Gerald Africa would

not help us obtain an interview with Ramona, it was decided that Brown would interview Gerald and at that time try once more to get his help in convincing Ramona to assist the investigation. I warned that an interview with Gerald would take days. He liked to talk, and he had a lot to say about the history of injustices against MOVE and the philosophy of John Africa.

The testimony of Birdie Africa would also provide the investigation with critical information about what happened inside the MOVE house during the gun battle and the fire. Birdie could also tell the commission how many people were in the house, who they were, and how many escaped or tried to escape. Birdie's father, Moses Ward, had taken custody of Birdie from the police. Birdie was represented by a lawyer because his father planned to file a lawsuit against the city for the emotional trauma and the physical injuries Birdie suffered. However, the commission was certain Birdie would testify; but under what circumstances?

Kauffman urged the commission to call Birdie as a witness during the public hearings. He was the only witness who would testify as to what happened inside the house, and the public should have an opportunity to hear him. There was no doubt that Birdie would be the most dramatic witness of the hearings. He could reveal details of the MOVE lifestyle. He could relate facts that might provide insights into the motivation which drove the adults who chose to perish in the fire rather than surrender. He might provide the only evidence that could absolve the MOVE adults of the accusations made against them.

Brown agreed with Kauffman, and the other commissioners also accepted the obvious need for Birdie to testify, but I objected to requiring him to testify at the public hearings. I did not want his face shown on television because I did not know who might decide to seek revenge or some other retribution against him. I did not want to compound the emotional trauma he had suffered by forcing him to face the bright lights and television cameras.

He had been burned. He had seen his playmates suffer. He had spent an entire day in the cold, wet basement of the house, listening to the gunfire of automatic weapons. He had endured and survived the explosion of the bomb. He had almost drowned in a pool of water as he tried to escape. I could not agree that the investigation, or any other endeavor, was important enough to add to the ordeal which had already marked his life.

Kauffman leaned forward as he replied. Birdie was too important a witness to exempt from testifying, he argued. He thought the commission could not justify requiring the police to testify and bypassing the only available eyewitness to what happened in the house. I almost leaped to my feet, but I managed to control that impulse, and I said, "You cannot equate Birdie with the police. Birdie was not a participant, he was an innocent bystander . . . a child dragged into an adults' conflict."

Father Washington joined my argument. He said the commission should not be guilty of the same inconsideration of children that was evident in the tragedy. Reverend Bronson agreed with Father Washington. We could not justify adding to Birdie's ordeal. Charisse Lillie suggested that we find a way to obtain Birdie's testimony without the distress of a public hearing. Ruth added that hauling Birdie before the lights and the cameras might make it more difficult to get full and complete testimony. He might be more comfortable, and therefore more responsive, in a friendlier setting.

Kauffman said he understood the problems testifying might cause Birdie, but the commission had to be impartial in its treatment of witnesses, and for the purposes of the investigation Birdie was just another witness. Brown wanted Birdie's testimony, but he did not believe the commission had to treat all witnesses the same. He reminded the commission that they had previously agreed that if there were witnesses who had legitimate reasons to fear for their personal safety if they testified in public, then the commission would hear them in an executive session. If a precedent was needed to treat Birdie differently from other witnesses, that decision should suffice.

When Monsignor Cullen also agreed that Birdie should be protected from testifying in public, Kauffman relented. There were several suggestions about how to obtain Birdie's testimony without taking it live before the cameras. I wanted to hear his testimony in an executive session without any cameras. Brown was first to object to that. He thought the public had to see Birdie as well as hear him. Kauffman and the others quickly endorsed Brown's position. After considering several alternatives it was decided to videotape Birdie's testimony.

The process of obtaining Birdie's testimony began with Brown meeting with him in the company of his father and his lawyer. Brown's gentle manner and quick, easy smile helped him to establish an excellent rapport with Birdie, and the videotaping was scheduled for Saturday, October 12, at 10 A.M. The commission accepted the conditions imposed by Birdie's father. Only Brown would be permitted to question Birdie, and he would refer to him by his Christian name, Michael Ward. The other commissioners who attended the interview would see it on video tape in another room, and they could provide Brown with questions they wanted him to ask Birdie. The interview would be interrupted by rest breaks of ten minutes every half hour, or as frequently as Birdie's father or Brown thought was necessary. Birdie would not be questioned about statements made by anyone involved in the tragedy. Birdie's lawyer would make an opening statement on behalf of Birdie and his father.

The lawyer read a prepared statement which outlined the efforts of Birdie's father to get custody of him while his mother was a member of MOVE and was rearing Birdie in the MOVE family. The statement tried to correct references in the news media which described Birdie as a MOVE member:

> He was throughout a member of what the psychologists would tell us was an expanded family unit consisting of one or more 'leaders'; one or more custodial 'parents' or parent figures including of course his natural mother, and children who in a real sense he would regard as his siblings. I emphasize these obvious points only in the context that to my surprise and disappointment, I have heard casual references to him as a 'MOVE member' or at least a confusion between his status as one of the children on the one hand, and the status of consenting adults on the other hand. Michael Ward (Birdie) was no more a member of MOVE than a child of Republican or Democratic parents would be styled by a particular party label.

Birdie was hospitalized from May 13 to May 28, and he was treated for burns and other injuries. In October he was still receiving medical treatment for the burns which healed with "profound keloid scarring and restriction of motion." The burns were of his back, abdomen, legs and face. His stature was that of a 9-year-old boy, but he was 13 when he was admitted to the hospital. His growth and development had probably been permanently compromised because of a protein-deficient diet. Psychological testing indicated that he also suffered from cognitive deprivation, and because he had never attended school, he was illiterate and not able to tell time. Despite his injuries, his deprivations and his suffering, as a witness he was intelligent and engaging. He was a handsome boy whose demeanor was completely cooperative and truthful. Women who saw the video tape of his testimony invariably said he was the kind of child they wanted to hug and adore. Without the dread-locks worn by the MOVE family, and dressed in the common attire of small boys, it was hard to imagine why anyone would harm him.

He testified for several hours in a soft, shy voice as he tried to overcome his limited vocabulary and painful memories to describe what he saw and heard. His description of gunfire as Conrad made the first attempt to surrender and escape the burning building was clear and convincing evidence that the MOVE members, in the basement garage of the burning house, were forced to chose between certain death by smoke and fire and the risk of death by police bullets. Only one member of the commission questioned the authenticity of Birdie's testimony. Kauffman disputed Birdie's description of the gunfire. He did not believe a 13-year-old boy, who had been listening to guns being fired for hours on May 13, could correctly identify the gunfire he heard as the MOVE members tried to escape.

When the video tape of Birdie's testimony was shown, it was the most poignant moment of the proceedings. Anyone could recognize familiar child-like qualities in him. He could have been one of the boys in any family, in any classroom, living on any street in Philadelphia. He was a powerful and eloquent representative of the children who were killed. Whatever the term "MOVE children" meant, it was erased by the video image of a shy, honest, cooperative boy telling the truth.

The volunteers began turning in reports of their interviews with residents of the 6200 block of Osage Avenue and the 6200 block of Pine Street. The Pine Street houses shared a common alley and driveway with the Osage Avenue houses. The residents' interviews confirmed most of the facts which were learned from official reports and memorandums. The residents' interview forms required the interviewer to ask if there was any aspect of the tragedy which they wanted the commission to investigate, and if the interviewee would be willing to testify before the commission.

Most of the residents wanted to know why the city waited so long before attempting to do anything about the MOVE house. They wanted the commission to determine if MOVE had dug tunnels under their streets. They wanted to know how many children were in the house and if the number of dead persons was confused because the police had mixed animal bones with human bones. They were almost unanimous in their criticism of the mayor for not acting sooner, but very few of them blamed him for the final outcome. In more than two hundred interviews less than ten of the interviewees expressed any sorrow for the lives that were lost. Perhaps the ordeal of the psychological warfare waged against them by the MOVE members left them emotionally numb. Perhaps they were trying too hard to overcome the scarred memories of the disaster they suffered to focus on the human dimensions of the tragedy. Perhaps they knew, for too long, that the confrontation had to end in violence and destruction, and therefore the event lost its significance.

Perhaps the MOVE members had become their enemies. Most of them were of the generation which had lived with war and tales of war since the mid-1940's. In news reports and in motion pictures the enemy was always killed and always deserved to die. They saw it live on television during the Vietnam war. No one mourned the death of enemies. The lost lives of enemies did not require grief or remorse. Their interviews indicated that for them it was a monumental disaster from which they may never recover, but the tragedy escaped them.

Since the commission's investigation began weeks after the events, gathering physical evidence presented special problems. The buildings were demolished. Rubble was disturbed or removed. Members of the Stakeout Unit had returned to the scene before dawn on May 14 and searched through the debris. When some of them were questioned, they said they were searching for souvenirs. The commission decided to retain its own forensic pathologist to identify the remains, its own expert on fire investigations to analyze the fire, and its own expert on explosives. These were routine decisions, but they produced the most definitive and startling evidence of the failures and motives of the public authorities involved.

In the commission's offices the filing cabinets were filled with documents, and there were boxes of more documents stacked in the corners of the rooms. Investigators had pages and pages of notes on everything from formal interviews to anonymous telephone calls. The commission decided that it would not give credence to any information that was not properly documented or was not sworn to under oath. Therefore the anonymous telephone calls and unsigned letters were brushed aside, but they were nevertheless disturbing. I received calls from people who whispered of seeing police officers shoot MOVE members in the alley and then drag their bodies back toward the MOVE house. There was the recurring story of the man who escaped the MOVE house and was taken away in a police vehicle. I was told that he was an undercover police officer living in the MOVE house. There were calls about police officers who were smiling as the MOVE house burned. Those calls were at least partially documented by a police video tape which the commission succeeded in enhancing to uncover background noises that would not be otherwise discernible.

A police camera crew was located on the second floor of a house on Osage Avenue, across from the MOVE house. They were videotaping the MOVE house as the roof was burning and then collapsed into the second floor. The flames were roaring and the heat was intense. The collapse of the roof caused bright orange-red flames to explode upward. At that moment no one knew if any of the adults or children in the house were on the second floor where the roof collapsed.

The police officers recorded on the video tape were laughing. One of them said, "They won't call the police commissioner a motherfucker anymore." Of all the facts established by the investigation that was the most damning. The search for facts had hit bedrock. The facts were that some of the police had come to Osage Avenue to kill—to kill by bullets or to kill by fire, but to kill nevertheless.

10

LIBERTY AND
JUSTICE

Organizations and individuals contacted the commission to express their outrage and grief over the death and destruction of May 13, and to express their fears. They were afraid that what had happened on Osage Avenue was symptomatic of a governmental proclivity to infringe upon fundamental rights of citizenship.

A week after the appointment of the commission, David Marion, Chancellor of the Philadelphia Bar Association, wrote to Brown, urging the commission to "address the issue of protection of civil rights prior to as well as during crises and what force society may utilize at what stage in attempting to secure compliance with its laws. While public officials must have the power to act decisively to protect public health and safety and to preserve order, they must also comply with the civil rights of all citizens and utilize force only to the extent necessary to those ends."

As the leader of Philadelphia's legal community, Marion wanted the commission to determine and define the civil rights of the Osage Avenue residents, the civil rights of MOVE members and their children, and the civil rights of police, firefighters and their families.

The famous admonition of Benjamin Franklin, 'Those who would forsake essential liberty for a little temporary safety deserve neither liberty nor safety," was implicit in each demand that the commission find some way to denounce any infringement of liberty or any threat to basic rights. There seemed to be a public consensus that Philadelphia could overcome the disaster of May 13, but it, and the nation, would be permanently damaged if the violations of liberty were not repaired.

A black father from West Philadelphia wrote, "What do fathers of black sons tell their sons of their duty to the nation? How can I teach him that he owes loyalty to his nation? Such is difficult enough considering this country's history with regards to blacks. A moment of truth has struck us. We are shown for what we are in fact, not what we say we are. We are shown to be a violent, intolerant, ignorant, brutal people. The libertarian thread of our social philosophy is now bare. We must search our very souls and ask what kind of country do we wish to live in. The real tragedy, however, will be that we will have become totally insensitive to the rights of others to live according to their creed, no matter how different from our own, and in becoming so insensitive will consider state repression and murder, such as occurred on May 13, acceptable."

The forces of government had won the violent battle on Osage Avenue, but they had not won the philosophical struggle at the core of the confrontation. The efforts of various officials to define the confrontation as one between the lawful authority of government and intransigent terrorists had failed. There was significant public concern about official deprivation of the liberty of MOVE members and preemptory denials of justice.

One woman who lived on South 57th Street, about six blocks from the Osage Avenue battleground, wrote to the mayor that the residents of Osage Avenue who claimed to be the victims of the MOVE members were also the tormentors of the MOVE members. She claimed residents of the MOVE house had worked hard to be good neighbors until the other residents of Osage Avenue began to mistreat the MOVE children. According to her, the MOVE members resorted to loudspeakers on the roof of their house because their neighbors regularly attacked them on radio and television talk shows. She also warned the mayor that the deprivation of MOVE's liberty was an encouragement to those forces in America that would also seek to destroy him.

The surviving spokesmen for the teachings of John Africa and the perpetuation of the MOVE lifestyle seized on the apparent philosophical contradictions inherent in the tragedy and tried to fashion a moral victory from the ashes of the MOVE house. Gerald Robert Ford Africa was the official spokesman for MOVE. He had been MOVE's Minister of Information for more than ten years. He was an intense, garrulous man who seemed to seek opportunities to lecture anyone in earshot of his voice. MOVE was his religion, and he was MOVE's preacher. Gerald Africa refused to testify publicly, but for three days—September 11, 12, and 13,—he talked to Brown and to Edward Scott, one of the commission's investigators, about MOVE and about the relationship between the May 13 battle and MOVE's ongoing conflict with police and other authorities.

One of the links between the tragedy and MOVE's prior relationships with the police was Officer Klein. He made the bomb, of powerful military explosives which were not authorized, and was one of several policemen who harassed MOVE members in 1974. At that time MOVE operated a fruit stand in front of its house, which was in the Powelton section of West Philadelphia at 309 North 33rd Street. Gerald Africa recalled that Klein was assigned to the 16th Police District and drove police car number 164. He said Klein regularly took fruit from MOVE's stand without paying for it until one of the female members of MOVE told him he could not do that. According to Gerald Africa, Klein became very angry, and when he was assigned to the night shift, he parked his police car in front of the MOVE house and turned on the siren. MOVE members watched him from their windows, and they could see him in the police car, laughing as the siren wailed.

Brown asked Gerald Africa why he was not in the house on Osage Avenue on May 13, and Gerald said he was awaiting a telephone call from Judge Robert Williams and Justice Robert N.C. Nix concerning a proposal to avoid violence.

Nix and Williams were two of three black appellate judges in Pennsylvania. Nix was Chief Justice of the Pennsylvania Supreme Court, and Williams was a judge of the Commonwealth Court, an intermediate appellate court. There was one other black appellate judge on the Pennsylvania Superior Court. Nix and Williams were Philadelphians. They had been lawyers in Philadelphia and were active in Philadelphia politics before they became judges. They knew about the violence and death that concluded the 1978 confrontation between MOVE and the police. On May 12, Williams talked to Gerald Africa about trying to settle the dispute on Osage Avenue. Gerald Africa said MOVE wanted a review of the trial records of the imprisoned MOVE members because they believed a scrutiny of the records would prove that the imprisoned MOVE members did not receive fair trials. Williams said that he would call Chief Justice Nix to request a further review of the trials. When he called Gerald Africa again he said that Nix was not available, but he would call the mayor to request that the city not take any action until he had an opportunity to talk to Justice Nix.

At that point the city was one telephone call away from avoiding the disaster, but Williams could not contact the mayor, who was out of town on a speaking engagement. Williams left a message requesting Justice Nix to return his telephone call, but the call was not returned. The mayor had gone to Virginia for a speaking engagement. He was out of the city for about three hours. When he returned the police operation on Osage Avenue was in progress. The telephone message Judge Williams left did not indicate that he wanted to discuss a possible negotiation of the crisis, so the mayor did not return Williams' call. He was concentrating on Osage Avenue.

In the afternoon of May 13, Williams called Gerald Africa to try to negotiate a settlement of the battle without the chief justice or the mayor. Gerald's confidence in the sincerity of Williams or anyone else connected with government was tenuous, and when Williams failed to reach Nix or the mayor, he was convinced negotiations were impossible. "I could have gotten the MOVE members out of the house," Gerald said. "However, I wanted to see, prior to making any moves in this direction, that the city was operating in an honest effort to assist us in our plight to remove members from jail."

Gerald refused to negotiate with Williams because there was no response from Nix or Goode, and because Charlie Burrus, a community activist who also had been trying to convince Gerald to negotiate, told him he had talked to the mayor on May 12. Gerald believed someone was lying to him about the mayor. On May 13, when he refused to negotiate, he believed there was still time to negotiate later. Despite his mistrust of lawful authorities, he did not imagine the lives of the MOVE members on Osage Avenue were in grave danger. Brown asked Gerald why the MOVE members did not leave the house when they saw the city was serious about evicting them. He said the members did not consider the police efforts to be that serious because they were certain the black community would not permit the police to assault the house. He also said the MOVE members believed the main complaint against them was their use of the loudspeakers, and they had not used them in many weeks.

There was a serious miscalculation of the situation by both sides. According to Gerald, the members of MOVE believed they were being singled out as a public nuisance. According to Sambor and the other leaders of the May 13 operation, they were armed and dangerous terrorists. Yet some of the MOVE members told the volunteers who tried to negotiate their surrender that they believed the police were prepared to kill them. Perhaps Gerald Africa was not in contact with the members in the house and did not know what they thought. Perhaps Gerald and the MOVE leaders thought they could tempt the city to the brink of violence and then negotiate, but they told the other members they intended to fight to the death.

Whatever the reasons for the miscalculation, it was based on an assumption that there were limits on the authority of the police and city officials. According to Gerald, MOVE believed the people who lived in the community could somehow intervene. That belief is consistent with the ideals of liberty and justice in America, but it is inconsistent with the reality. When the people, massed at the scene, shouted their protests of the assault and the raging fire, they were silenced. They were silenced by pleas not to become unruly because the police might turn their weapons on them. The bitter reality of May 13 was that once the police forces were unleashed without effective controls, liberty and justice ended at the muzzles of their weapons.

Their weapons were aimed at a group which believed in liberty without any limits. That was the philosophical struggle which could not be resolved with guns. Who was right on Osage Avenue? Not who was lawful or unlawful, but who was right? John Africa taught his disciples, "When your reference is right you don't have to run from it, hide from it, make excuses for it, don't have to make no deals, negotiate no compromise, involve yourself in no damn concession."

John Africa's sister, LaVern Sims, wrote a 33-page letter to the commission in November, which was the brief for MOVE's argument for liberty and justice. She wrote, "MOVE's stand was right as the sun that shines even behind the clouds. And it is sad that we as a people have to stand up for right but be shot down, bombed into fragmented pieces that once was a form of life with blood running through the veins of life. Life and freedom and justice of God that cost nothing, that man has made us pay for with death. What have we as black people done, that we be rewarded with such agony, suffering and excruciating pain for our labor?"

She reviewed all of the complaints and the legal warrants that were the official provocations for May 13, and argued that even if they were all valid they did not justify the manpower, weaponry and combat tactics which resulted in the tragedy.

"They said it was profanity. They said it was garbage. They said it was because of threats, because of parole violations, bench warrants. They said it was because of a bunker. They said it was because of a bullhorn that's bullshit. On May 13, 1985 the manpower MOVE was faced with wasn't for nothing. The arsenal wasn't for nothing, the steel bullets wasn't for nothing, the Uzis wasn't for nothing; the silencers wasn't for nothing and that bomb wasn't for nothing. They had a reason for bringing all they had and that reason was John Africa."

For Sims it was not an eviction or an arrest that brought official forces to Osage Avenue; they came for a crucifixion. Once more, in the never-ending twists of history, the forces of lawful authority were used to kill a message of religious truth, to end the yearning for limitless liberty and to abort the life of justice. She argued that John Africa was not just a man, he was the power of his truth, an indestructible power that blows like a blizzard. Like so many religious prophets before him, John Africa—and his disciples—learned that liberty and justice are not extant as cosmic values or as innate qualities of human nature. Liberty and justice are the products of the political, social and economic systems which define them. The rhetorical phrases which announce their existence, such as the claim that Americans have inalienable rights to life, liberty and the pursuit of happiness, are never definitive.

In every society which claims to be free there is at best a contentious relationship between individual liberty and government authority. The legal, social and political networks by which the contentions are arbitrated provide the stability which is essential to modern civilization. As the contentions between liberty and authority work their way through the networks they are muted, modified and resolved. The system works when there is a viable compact among the people to submit their contentions to the networks and to rely on the result of their operations.

When the American colonies perceived intolerable inequities in the legal, social and political networks which linked them to the English throne, they decided no longer to rely on the networks of the colonial system. They fractured their compact with the English nation—they rebelled. The liberty accorded their colonial status was not enough. The justice dispensed by a distant monarch was not fair. They renounced the authority of the English king by claiming that God's authority entitled them to limitless liberty and perfect justice.

Even as Thomas Jefferson wrote the American pronouncement of liberty and justice, everyone knew it did not apply to women, black people, native Americans, indentured servants and anyone who was not wealthy enough to enforce liberty and justice through the courts or strong enough to enforce them with weapons. MOVE's demand that liberty and justice must be truthfully defined conflicted with centuries of their hypocritical definition. As products, liberty and justice were more plentiful in America in 1985, but they still had a price. Their application to daily endeavors was still strained through the hypocrisy inherent in social, economic, political and legal orders.

Philadelphia, which in 1776 had been the symbolic birthplace of liberty and justice in America, had become in 1985 the disfiguring birthmark on liberty and justice. Around the world and across the nation there was concern that the battle of Osage Avenue was proof that John Africa was right about the "system."

Nothing of value which was consumed by the conflict could be restored. Rebuilt houses would not re-establish the homes which were destroyed, and the lost lives were gone. The commission was perceived as the instrument for limiting the losses to the property and the lives. The commission was saddled with the burden of restoring the appearance of liberty and justice. Whatever else it did, the commission had to remove the birthmark revealed in the flickering light of the firestorm that obliterated the homes and eleven lives on Osage Avenue.

The irony of the restoration drama imposed upon the commission was that the central figure was the first black mayor of Philadelphia. Human error and tyranny have not been the exclusive defects of any racial group, and there was ample historical precedent to support Mayor Goode's role. But in America black people had been the moral force and the human drive behind struggles to improve and perfect liberty and justice. Black people were the nonviolent victims of the movement for civil rights and human dignity which shamed the nation into a better definition of liberty and justice. They were the human symbols of the deprivation of liberty and the denial of justice. A black skin had achieved a noble place in the national conscience. The nightmarish extremes of American racism had engendered enough guilt, frustration and decency to propel the national life closer to a society of citizens of equal standing.

Philadelphia was the last major American city to elect a black person as its mayor. Birmingham, Alabama, Atlanta, Georgia and

New Orleans, Louisiana—Southern cities which had been strongholds of racial oppression—joined the cathartic wave of political change before Philadelphia. W. Wilson Goode's election as mayor of Philadelphia meant that the sacred birthplace of American liberty and justice was managed by a representative of America's most oppressed ethnic group.

The commission gathered facts and planned its hearings mindful of the philosophical implications of Mayor Goode's role. The unspoken question which must have dogged the minds and consciences of each of the commission members as it dogged mine was, "Could we help to heal the wounds and remove the blemish from liberty and justice without also demanding the removal of Philadelphia's first black mayor?"

As the date for beginning the hearings drew near, the meetings of the commission became more and more absorbed with determining the mayor's role in the tragedy and also with urging the commission to strive for unanimity in its conclusions. In one manner or another, one or more of the commissioners found an excuse to mention the need for unanimity at each of the meetings before the hearings began. There was a sense among them that their judgments would be more valid, and their individual roles in arriving at them more respected, if their final pronouncement was unanimous.

I disagreed with the consensus that unanimity was essential. I argued that the only important result was the honest assessment of the facts by each commissioner, and if that resulted in eleven separate opinions then so be it. The other commissioners were openly disturbed by my position. Brown telephoned me to suggest that above all else the commission's conclusion should not be based on a racially divided vote of the commissioners. There was the possibility that the six black commissioners, who were a majority of the commission would issue a report absolving the black mayor who had appointed them, and the five white commissioners would issue a minority report blaming the mayor for the tragedy. Such a result would have compounded the tragedy and extended the trauma of the spring of 1985. The possibility had to exist because each commissioner had to decide and vote as an individual, and a six-to-five racial split was one of the conceivable outcomes.

Consciously trying to avoid that result was more damaging to the integrity of the commission's work than merely accepting its existence as one of many possibilities. I would not be bound by a silent understanding that the commission would avoid a racial split in its voting or in its final report because I believed that if that happened it would not happen for racial reasons.

The commission members had diverse backgrounds and perspectives, but they quickly established a common interest in the value of liberty and justice. Kauffman made it clear that he would not agree that rank-and-file police officers had any malevolence in their actions, and that racial considerations were not implicated in the tragedy, but he abhorred the deaths of the children. His face was flushed with anger and his voice weakened with emotion when he spoke of their deaths. He sincerely wanted justice for them, and he wanted someone to pay for the deprivation of their liberty. He would not believe that police officers, who were "following orders," could be at fault.

Cooke and Ruth were the primary reasons I knew there would not be a racial split in the voting. They shared with the black members on the commission a desire to make the "system" work for everyone. They had worked and succeeded within the structure of American society. They had benefited from its great principles. They had enjoyed the fullness of American liberty and justice, and they were personally offended by the exclusion of any of their compatriots from its blessings.

The black members had also succeeded within the system, but they had fought for every inch. They had overcome the racial barriers to their success. They had outmaneuvered the subtle exclusions. They had passed the stiffest tests. They had so much invested in breaking into the system they wanted it to work. They wanted the black generations which followed them to negotiate their paths with less trouble. The racial differences on the commission were not strong enough to supersede the common commitment to the perfection and the enjoyment of American liberty and justice. That common commitment was the most valid criticism of the commission because it meant that MOVE's version of liberty was inconceivable. It meant that no matter where the facts fixed responsibility, the philosophical struggle could not be resolved in favor of the teachings of John Africa. If liberty could be limitless, and if justice could be perfect and free of human influence, then there could have been fair consideration of MOVE's philosophy. The hearings could have examined the teachings of John Africa and compared his versions of the truth to those truths represented by everything the commissioners believed in.

That inquiry could have taken months, maybe years. It would

have required acrimonious debate and painstaking historical re-
search. It would have required opening minds and testing sacred
values. It would have required questioning the unquestionable
foundations of American society. There was neither the time nor
the inclination to initiate such an analysis. The trauma of the
tragedy lingered within the Philadelphia community throughout
the oppressive heat and humidity of the summer. The warehouses
filled with clothing and furniture, contributed to help the displaced
residents of Osage Avenue, and a million-dollar relief fund had not
assuaged the anguish.

The fresh greenness of the spring was transformed into a
spectrum of autumn foliage, and the commissioners knew they
had to begin the public hearings before winter. They believed that
their credibility and the integrity of their investigation were inextricably linked to their ability to hold the public hearings without
delay. They concentrated on determining the facts. The investigation was focused on who did what, when and where, and who said
what to whom about which subject. As the inquiry into the facts
unraveled the confusion and the cloud of concealment that surrounded many aspects of the tragedy, there were implications and
innuendoes which touched the broader concerns of liberty and
justice.

During the commission's meetings Ruth insisted that the
investigation develop the facts of life for the neighbors of the MOVE
house. He wanted to make certain their story was heard by the
public. He wanted the city to understand what it was like to live
with the intrusions and discomforts that were visited upon them.
Brown, Kauffman and Lytton wanted to review MOVE's philosophy
to determine if it had changed from one of nonviolence to one of
terrorism and violence from 1976 to 1985. No one suggested that
the commission's inquiry should include an effort to try to understand MOVE's philosophy and its influence on the events that
culminated on May 13.

The fact-finding parameters imposed on, and accepted by, the
commission provided justification for avoiding the moral and
philosophical explications of the evidence, but the final, historical
judgment of the commission's work might not accept that justification. As the commission moved inexorably to the public hearings,
its investigation was slanted to judge MOVE's existence and its
philosophy without trying to understand either. The resources
available to the commissioners and the time they could reasonably
use did not allow for more than what they planned. They were

faced with the limitations imposed on every tribunal which must determine its judgment within the context of the truths of the society which empowered it.

The commission had its first working meeting on June 8, and it decided to begin the public hearings on October 8. Eleven lives had been ended, and misery had engulfed more than two hundred families; how could it be understood in four months? I concluded that it could not be understood, and therefore the commission risked the same historical judgment that condemned the Romans who tried the Christians, the ecclesiastical courts which tried the heretics, and the colonial tribunals which condemned witches. If the self-evident truths of our system were invalid and John Africa's truths were valid, then, inevitably, our truths would fade and his would survive.

Whenever there are too few facts or other evidence to validate a proposition, then it can only be validated by faith. I prepared for the public hearings, confident that liberty and justice would not suffer because we did not try to understand the teachings of John Africa. The system he deplored provided liberty and justice. I had faith in the system and not in him.

11

BIG FOUR FINALE

More than four hundred journalists applied for press credentials by the time the public hearings began on October 8, 1985. They represented news organizations throughout the United States and foreign countries including the Soviet Union. WHYY TV-12, the Public Broadcasting System affiliate in Philadelphia, televised the hearings live from the main auditorium of its building, located on Race Street, between 6th and 7th Streets, three blocks north of Independence Hall. One of several buildings erected as part of the 1976 bicentennial celebration of the signing of the Declaration of Independence, it housed a museum of American history. After the celebration it was donated to WHYY by the city.

It was a red brick structure, in deference to the red bricks of Independence Hall. The main entrance to the building was on Sixth Street, in a plate glass wall which reflected the dazzling morning sun. There was also an entrance, from Race Street, directly into the auditorium. The public entered the auditorium through a police check-point and metal detector at the Race Street entrance. The commissioners and the staff entered through a back entrance that was reached from an alley to Sixth Street. They were identified by a police officer at the gate to the alley and again by one stationed at a small table inside the back door. Security was tight and unobtrusive. There were a few shouted protests from the audience on the first day of hearings, and one or two disorderly individuals on other days, but for the most part the auditorium was less than half filled. The real audience was on the receiving end of the television transmission. Within the metropolitan area, daily routines and daily soap operas were superseded by telecasts of the commission's hearings.

Housewives, college students, nightshift workers and the unemployed studied the images on their TV screens, or listened on small radios, as they tried to determine who among the witnesses was telling the truth, and if the commission was asking the right questions. The hearings were conducted on the stage, located at the base of the 45-degree decline of the auditorium floor from street level. The commissioners were seated behind two of three tables arranged so that the front of the stage was the fourth side of a rectangle. The table to the right side of the stage was the witness table.

The longest table faced the front of the stage and the audience. Seated at that table from right to left were Henry Ruth, Father Washington, Bruce Kauffman, Julia Chinn, Monsignor Edward Cullen, Reverend Audrey Bronson, Carl Singley, Bill Brown and Bill Lytton. At the table on the left, facing the witness table which was across the stage, was Neil Welch, seated next to Lytton, Charisse Lillie and Todd Cooke, and I was seated at the end.

In the center of the incomplete rectangle formed by the tables was a large model of the houses adjoining the MOVE house on both sides, the MOVE house itself and the driveway and alley behind the houses. The investigator who operated the computer on which the evidentiary documents and exhibits were stored was seated at a small table directly behind Lytton and Brown. TV cameras were positioned to focus on the commissioners, the witness table and the model. WHYY agreed not to focus a camera on the audience to avoid encouraging demonstrations. However, they retained the right to televise any action in the audience which they thought was newsworthy.

The "Green Room," which had walls painted dark gray, was assigned to the commissioners. We met there before and after the daily hearings and during lunch breaks. When the eleven commissioners and three other people were in the room, it was too crowded for everyone to sit. It was impossible to say anything in the room which was not overheard by everyone in the room. Every member of the commission attended almost every hearing. The hearings began at 10 A.M. and often continued until after 5 P.M., Monday through Thursday. Commission members tried to maintain their occupational and other duties before 9 A.M., after 6 P.M. and during luncheon breaks.

It was a grueling pace which extended the emotional, intellectual and physical endurance of the commissioners. Except for Kauffman, who always made himself available to reporters and almost daily made some public comment on the proceedings, the commissioners operated as if they were a jury hearing evidence at a trial. They avoided news reporters and anyone else who tried to discuss the evidence as it was developing. Commenting on a single day's testimony or the testimony of certain witnesses, without the benefit of the complete testimony, could lead to misinterpretations and distortions.

The hearings were planned to provide a historical perspective and a chronological presentation of the events which preceded the tragedy, as well as details of what happened on May 13. In his opening statement to commence the hearings, Brown tried to minimize the importance of conflicting testimony. He said, "As the testimony develops we, the commission, and you, the public, will be hearing intricate, and at times dramatic, detail as the witnesses tell us what they did and what they knew and what they observed. Some accounts may appear to be in conflict, and this is normal; some differences may simply be a matter of differing points of view. Withhold your judgments until all the facts are in."

As the testimony developed, the audience learned that between direct questions and responsive answers there were various opportunities for evasive responses which allowed witnesses to avoid answering questions without committing that level of falsehood which could be defined as perjury. The lexicon of evasion included responses such as, "I don't recall," or "Not to my knowledge," or "No one told me specifically," or "My impression of what was said was . . . ," or "I remember but I can't recall who said it," or responding to a question with a statement about events other than those included in the question.

Brown's opening statement was prudent advice, but the conflicting accounts of Goode, Brooks, Sambor and Richmond— whom the commissioners referred to as the "Big Four"—were so profound they required a change in the plan for the hearings. Most of all, the public wanted to hear what the Big Four had to say about the tragedy. The commission knew that the success of its work depended, in part, on maintaining the public's interest in the hearings, and that meant getting the Big Four on camera as soon as it was feasible to present their testimony. They could not be presented out of context, and they could not be Delayed beyond the public's limit of anticipating their testimony. The timing had to be right.

Mayor Goode began his testimony on October 11, 1985, the fourth day of the hearings, and returned for the entire day on

October 15. Brooks' testimony consumed October 16, and Sambor used October 17 and 18. The testimony of the first three of the Big Four was related to the testimony preceding them regarding the history, planning and implementation of the assault on the MOVE house. Richmond's testimony was primarily related to the fire, and therefore he did not testify until October 29 and 30. By hearing Goode, Brooks and Sambor on successive days, the commission thought it would have ample opportunities to compare their testimony. However, by the end of Sambor's first appearance, the commissioners realized that the Big Four had to be summoned to testify jointly about their conflicting versions of what happened. It was a decision which the commission might not have agreed to if they had not heard the litany of ineptness and failure that was revealed during the first week of the hearings.

Even after that depressing testimony there was concern among the commissioners that requiring the Big Four to explain their conflicts in each other's presence implied that the conflicts were caused by deliberate falsehoods. I was one of the commissioners who believed someone was lying, and the failure of the commission to require the Big Four to testify jointly would destroy its credibility. After the first week, the original plan to end the hearings in October was amended. The hearings would continue into November to allow enough time for the Big Four finale. That decision, more than anything else, cast the commission as the instrument of the public will. We hauled the leaders before the cameras and made them explain themselves to the people. Our judgment of their conduct would come later, but our greatest contribution to validating our work, and to restoring public confidence, was in demonstrating that the leaders could be held accountable.

Conflicting testimony among the Big Four was most pronounced and significant in six areas. They were:

1. Delay

   Was there an official city policy of nonconfrontation which permitted the MOVE family to disobey the law? Who was responsible for the policy?

2. Lost Opportunities

   Could the Big Four have avoided the tragedy by better planning and better decision-making?

3. Gas And Bullets

Was there dangerously excessive utilization of gas and weaponry?

4. Explosives

Was there sufficient control and expertise to warrant the use of Explosives as part of the operation?

5. The Bomb

Who was involved in the decisions to make and drop the bomb?

6. Letting The Bunker Burn

Who was responsible for the decisions that caused the fire and prevented firefighters from fighting the fire until it was too late?

DELAY

Indecision is never accidental or acceptable in the operations of government. When there is a crisis or a serious problem, indecision is dangerous and stupid. Every one of the leaders of Philadelphia's government who testified said they knew about the 1978 confrontation between members of MOVE and the police. They knew the 1978 episode ended with violence and death. They knew MOVE had threatened the same result if there was a confrontation on Osage Avenue.

They knew, yet they watched and waited as MOVE members armed themselves and fortified their house. The mayor, and various members of his administration—including the heads of the licenses and inspections, police and water departments testified that they Delayed in taking action to enforce the laws which were broken by MOVE members because of a policy of nonconfrontation with MOVE.

Mayor Goode testified that the policy, which was the basis for Delay, "evolved" during the administration of his predecessor, William Green. Goode served as managing director under Green, but he resigned early in 1983 to seek election as mayor. According to him, the policy evolved after he resigned, but he agreed with it and adopted it when he took office in January 1984. By the spring of 1984, Goode believed the Osage Avenue situation was dangerously explosive. He testified, "It was my view and it was my policy which I in fact carried over from the Green administration. I want to make sure you understand that I was fully aware and saw this as a sound policy decision, that I did not want the risk of any inspector going to their house, pushing a button, that could end up with a loss of lives, of that inspector, of children in their neighborhood, of civilians in that neighborhood and therefore I wanted any approach to solving the problem at 6221 Osage Avenue to be done at an appointed time when we could carefully think out and plan what ought to be done."

The mayor testified about Green's involvement in the policy of Delay in the afternoon of October 11, 1985. When the commissioners gathered in the Green Room at the end of the mayor's testimony, Brown received a telephone call from Green. Most of us standing near Brown could hear Green's voice.Brown covered the telephone mouthpiece and said softly, "It's Bill Green . . . he sounds hysterical. He's demanding that we give him a chance to testify to refute what the mayor said about his policy on MOVE."

I responded that we should not change our schedule of witnesses to accommodate him. We had provided in our rules for persons who wanted to reply to unfavorable testimony. They could submit an affidavit of their version of the events. I said to Brown, "Tell him to send us an affidavit."

The other commissioners in the room indicated their agreement. Brown carefully explained that we could not interrupt the hearings for Green's response to the mayor. If we did that it could establish a precedent that would obligate the commission to allow everyone who was criticized by a witness to testify in response. Brown told the former mayor to send the commission an affidavit.

Green wrote a letter to the commission and called a press conference to announce his reply to the mayor's testimony. In his letter Green said he was not questioning the mayor's veracity in his statement that the policy of non- enforcement of the law evolved during Green's administration of the city. Green referred to Goode's testimony on October 12, when he named city department commissioners William Marrazzo, Raymond Tate and Eugene Cliett "as his sources" for the claim that the policy began during Green's tenure. Then, in a direct attack on Goode's veracity, Green wrote, "All three commissioners have personally told me that never to anyone, at anytime, did they indicate such a policy to be my policy or Green administration policy."

Green insisted that it was his policy to enforce the law in all areas without exception. His specific policy with regard to MOVE was "to intervene as soon as possible if MOVE action mandated force. To me, one lesson of 1978 was to move with care but swiftly. Allowing a MOVE buildup was dangerous as far as I was concerned."

Green was sworn in as mayor in January 1980, sixteen months after the August 8, 1978 confrontation between MOVE and the police. On August 4, 1981, eighteen months into the Green administration, nine MOVE members were sentenced to prison terms of thirty to one hundred years each for the murder of a police officer during the confrontation.

MOVE members moved into 6221 Osage Avenue in 1982, and by the end of 1983, while Green was mayor, they had begun profane nighttime harangues on loudspeakers, and they had made oral and written threats to harm various officeholders and to kill any police officer or other city official who tried to enter the MOVE house. The other residents of Osage Avenue had met with public officials and sent petitions to mayor Green outlining MOVE's violations of the peace and tranquillity on Osage Avenue and also violations of various city health and building codes. If Green had a policy of enforcing the law without exception and of acting swiftly with regard to MOVE, it was not communicated to his subordinates, who did not enforce the law and who did nothing about MOVE.

In the end it did not matter whether Goode or Green was correct about the origin of the policy which ignored MOVE's challenge to lawful authority and destroyed the home life of the residents of Osage Avenue—the result was Delay. Neither mayor demonstrated the leadership the voters deserved. For good or ill, the administration of local government is a reflection of its leadership. When indecision, inaction and indifference paralyze or subvert the normal functions of government, the mayor is responsible. If he intended a different result then he should have produced a different result.

When Mayor Goode, Managing Director Brooks and Police Commissioner Sambor, took office in 1984 the situation on Osage Avenue required action. During the joint testimony of the Big Four, Sambor repeated his previous testimony that he recommended police action against MOVE between October 1984 and February 1985. He recalled recommending action to Brooks and that Brooks agreed with him but indicated there were other considerations which prevented taking action. Brooks testified that he did not recall receiving a recommendation from Sambor. He contended that if he had received a recommendation of action from Sambor, he would have discussed it with the mayor.

The mayor said no one mentioned action against MOVE between October 1984 and February 1985, and if they had there was no reason why he would not have approved taking action against the MOVE house. Brooks did recall that Sambor mentioned there was construction on the roof of the MOVE house, but it was not described as a bunker or other fortification. Brooks claimed the construction on the roof was not referred to as a "bunker" until the spring of 1985. According to Sambor, he never discussed his recommendation to take action with the mayor because he did not initiate communications with the mayor. He could only initiate communications with the managing director, who decided what was to be referred to the mayor.

The conflict between Sambor and Brooks is further complicated because as early as May 1984, the mayor met with the U.S. attorney about his problems with MOVE. In August of 1984, the mayor discussed MOVE with the city solicitor, Barbara Mather, and asked her under what circumstances the city could take custody of the children living in the MOVE house. Goode held weekly cabinet meetings, and his cabinet included the city solicitor and the managing director. Brooks never mentioned his 1984 discussions with Sambor to the mayor, and the city solicitor testified that between August 1984 and April 1985 the mayor never discussed MOVE with her. There was no explanation forthcoming from the mayor as to why he met with the U.S. attorney in May 1984, when he discussed taking custody of the children living in the MOVE house, but he did not discuss the problem at a cabinet meeting or any other meeting of his administration before the spring of 1985.

There also was no explanation from Sambor as to why he did not tell Brooks about the tactical advantage and the potential danger to police represented by the structure which he knew was being built on the roof of the MOVE house in October 1984. His excuse was that he did not know the extent of the fortification, even though he realized it provided its occupants with a tactical advantage. Considering that construction on the roof of the MOVE house began after the police show of force in August 1984, as well as the history of violent encounters with MOVE members and their threats to kill public officials and anyone who tried to enter their house, Sambor's excuse was ludicrous.

The reason most often given by the mayor and Brooks for

delaying action to solve the problem was the lack of any legal authority to act. It was the reason for delay which the mayor gave when he met with elected officials who wanted him to take some action, and which he also gave to the residents of the 6200 block of Osage when they met with him to demand action in July 1984. The conflicts between their testimony and the facts about their legal authority were astounding.

The mayor steadfastly contended that his understanding of the absence of legal authority was based on a memorandum which he received from the district attorney in June 1984. The district attorney sent a covering letter with his memorandum, with copies to Brooks, on June 22, 1984. In the covering letter he wrote, "I would reiterate . . . it is imperative to do something as quickly as possible before the situation grows even worse." The memorandum stated that there were outstanding arrest warrants against Frank James Africa and Ramona Africa. The commission obtained records and testimony from Yvonne B. Haskins, Philadelphia Regional Supervisor of the Pennsylvania Parole Board, which established that the parole board issued an arrest warrant for Frank James Africa on June 6, 1984. When the parole board sought the assistance of the Philadelphia Police Department to arrest Frank Africa, they were requested to delay executing the warrant.

When Sambor testified individually on October 17, 1985, he said that members of the police Civil Affairs Unit told him about the warrant for Frank Africa in June or July of 1984, and within a few days he told Brooks. When Brooks testified individually on October 16, 1985, he said he did not think he was aware of a warrant for the arrest of Frank Africa in 1984.

When the Big Four testified jointly on November 6, 1985, Sambor repeated his claim that he told Brooks of the warrant in June or July of 1984. Brooks amended his prior testimony. He said, "I was aware that there was a parole violator. I am not certain that I was aware that there was a warrant."

Only Sambor remembered that they knew about the warrant which provided the same legal authority the city finally relied on. Sambor could afford to remember because once he reported the existence of the warrant to Brooks, who was his superior, he had no further responsibility for the decision to take action to execute the warrant. If the mayor and Brooks admitted knowledge of the warrant in June or July 1984, they could not rely on the lack of legal authority as an excuse for not acting sooner than they did.

Perhaps the mayor and Brooks did not understand the legal significance of the district attorney's advice that there were "outstanding warrants" against Frank and Ramona in June 1984. However, they did not get an evaluation or comment on the memorandum from the city solicitor who was their lawyer and the proper person to give them legal advice.

The only reasonable explanation is that everyone involved knew about the warrant for Frank Africa in June or July 1984, but at that time they were hopeful the problem would go away, or that some agreement could be reached with the MOVE members, so they ignored the warrants. It is not likely they were seriously concerned about the legal rights of the MOVE members, because when they decided to assault the MOVE house, and they obtained additional warrants for that purpose, they also ignored those warrants.

The Big Four did not bother to read the arrest warrants upon which they based their assault on Osage, and consequently did not know what degree of force they could legally use. Sambor said he knew the warrants were properly issued and they listed felonies and misdemeanors, and that was sufficient. He was wrong. The degree of force which a police officer may use is related to the specific crime which has been committed and the surrounding circumstances. Brooks should have read the charges stated in the warrants to determine how much force he would permit Sambor to use. Brooks didn't bother to read the warrants, and no one told him about them. Richmond also failed to read the warrants, and only knew they included felony charges. Not only did the mayor fail to read the warrants, he also failed to meet with Brooks, Sambor and Richmond to discuss the legal basis for the plan. That failure prompted the following question to the Big Four from commissioner Lillie: "When the mayor, the former managing director and the police commissioner testified previously, I asked all of you whether or not in the planning stages you had discussed the legal implications of using force in a situation such as you had at 6221 Osage where there were persons in the house who were not the subjects of arrest and search warrants and where you had children, and my understanding of your testimony is that none of you really recalled this kind of specific legal discussion even though you at times did talk about the question of use of force. And the question that I have for the three of you is why was this never discussed in a formal kind of way?"

I sat on the edge of my seat as I looked across the stage into the faces of Goode, Brooks and Sambor. I expected some expression of contrition, some recognition of the extent of their negligence. I expected acknowledgment of their duty to protect the children even as they used deadly force to arrest adults. I was disappointed. Each of them said they could not answer Lillie. Sambor said they discussed the presence of adults and children in the house, but no legal objections were raised. As far as he was concerned, once he received the warrants, there were no impediments.

Brooks said he didn't know why the innocent women and children were not considered. He attended meetings on May 3 and 7, 1985, which included lawyers from the district attorney's office and the city solicitor's office. They did not discuss the degree of force which could be used. He added that the plan for the assault had not been formulated prior to those meetings.

Mayor Goode said, "I don't think, commissioner, that we can answer that. At least I can't answer that. It was just simply not one of the things that came into my mind that I had posed a question about it. And therefore I don't have any explanation beyond the fact that it never came up specifically in those terms."

They did not think about the innocent residents of the MOVE house, and they did not discuss their legal rights, because they did not care about them. The Big Four had unleashed the Stakeout Unit with their heavy weapons and The Bomb Disposal Unit with bags of Explosives without considering the legal basis for exposing small children, and adults who were not accused of any crime, to the grave dangers which were visited on the MOVE house.

LOST OPPORTUNITIES

Along the path to the disastrous confrontation there were opportunities to avoid it or to mitigate the tragedy of it. The decision to use force should have been considered in the context of the police department's relationship with the MOVE organization. The death of Officer Ramp during the 1978 confrontation was an important factor of that relationship.

The mayor and Brooks testified about a meeting in early May, attended by Councilman Lucien Blackwell, the district attorney and the Big Four. There was a discussion of selecting the police who would be assigned to the Osage operation. The mayor and Brooks recalled that Councilman Blackwell vehemently argued against assigning any police officer who took part in the 1978 confrontation. He was concerned that someone might seek to avenge Officer Ramp.

According to Brooks and the mayor, Goode instructed Sambor to hand-pick the men who were assigned to the Osage operation. Sambor said he was at the meeting, but he did not recall the discussion by Blackwell, and he was certain the mayor did not tell him to hand-pick the men. After the mayor and Brooks testified, Sambor was offered a chance to change his testimony, but he remained certain the mayor had not instructed him to hand-pick the men.

Another critical opportunity was lost when Sambor failed to "pick up" the children who lived in the MOVE house before the operation began. Sambor admitted receiving instructions from Mayor Goode to pick up the children, but he contradicted the mayor's testimony about when the instructions were given to him. The mayor testified that he told Sambor on May 7 to pick up the children. When the mayor and Sambor were asked if their different recollections of when the instructions were given could be reconciled, the mayor said, 'The order took place on May 7. I was very much aware, however, that the order could not be carried out or implemented until such time as the city solicitor had gone into court and gotten permission to do so. It is my understanding that in fact took place on the evening of May 9, 1985."

Sambor was certain that the mayor did not tell him to pick up the children until the evening of May 9 or the morning of May 10. When Sambor heard the mayor insist that he had given the order on May 7, Sambor said that there had been discussions earlier than May 9 about the possibility of picking up the children if a court granted permission, but he stuck to his assertion that no order was given before May 9.

The concern expressed by the mayor and Sambor about the legalities involved in picking up the children, when they were planning to attack the MOVE house with massive force, was indicative of the focus on bureaucratic procedures that obscured their insights into the substance of what they intended to do. Since failure to pick up the children could endanger their lives, violation of the legal technicalities in order to protect their lives would not have been a serious offense. But the procedures confused and confounded the intention to pick up the children.

On May 9, Sambor telephoned Dr. Irene Pernsley, commissioner of the city's Department of Health and Human Services, and asked her if she could pick up the children. She asked one question, "Are they MOVE children?" Then she said they could not be taken into custody by her department if they were not victims of abuse or neglect. There were no such reports. She did not ask Sambor if the children were in danger of bodily harm, and he did not mention the plan to attack the house where the children lived.

On the same day Sambor met with Assistant city solicitor Ralph Teti to discuss the legality of picking up the children. Although Sambor did not tell Dr. Pernsley about the plan for May 13, he did tell Teti. Teti told him the children could be picked up if they were in imminent danger of harm. Teti immediately made arrangements with the Family Court to have a judge available on a 24-hour basis to authorize picking up the children. By the end of the day on May 9, Sambor knew he could pick up the children and a judge was available, to issue an order to do so. Sambor said he ordered Captain Shanahan to instruct his men, who had the MOVE house under surveillance, to pick up the children at the first opportunity.

Detective Matthews and Officers Draper, Mitchell and Jones received the order from Captain Shanahan on the morning of May 10. They were not told about plans to assault the MOVE house on May 13, and therefore did not understand the significance of the order. Moreover the order was given to them orally, and they were not certain what the order meant. They did not think there was a deadline for picking up the children, and they thought they were only to get the children who lived on Osage Avenue and not other children who from time to time visited the Osage Avenue house from other MOVE houses.

They were on duty on Saturday, May 11, when a blue car driven by a MOVE member stopped at the police barrier which had been placed at each end of the 6200 block of Osage. There were children in the car, but the officers removed the barrier and permitted the children to enter the house. If they had been told that in two days police officers armed with automatic weapons and explosives would attack the house, they would have taken the children out of the car. Sambor's insistence on secrecy and his fear that MOVE members were able to learn about police plans limited the information given to the officers who could have picked up the children and saved their lives.

More than any other aspect of the tragedy, the failure to protect the children evoked moral outrage from Kauffman. It was common ground he shared with the other commissioners. The deep quality of Kauffman's voice was thinned by emotion as he leaned forward, stared into Sambor's eyes and asked, "Why, why did you not, when you learned that the children hadn't yet been picked up, decide to put off the operation on the 13th, order that your order be put in writing in unmistakable, unambiguous language, order a 24-hour surveillance of the premises, indeed, even including trailing the car in which the children often rode and give some additional effort to picking up those children before the armed confrontation . . . ?"

It was a rambling question which revealed Kauffman's angry frustration and his incredulity at how casually the leaders of the operation considered the danger to the children. The obvious premise on which his question was based was his own sense of compassion. Without regard to the legal and other official imperatives which should have dictated greater concern for the safety of children, Kauffman was stunned that there was not enough compassion among the leaders to guarantee the children's safety.

The mayor answered Kauffman's question by equating the opportunity to protect the children with the importance of the tactics of the operation. He said, "Mr. Justice, I can say to you that once we had telegraphed to the MOVE organization the possibility of a confrontation, that it was my view that those children would not leave the house, that once we had started to evacuate the homes, we have in fact committed ourselves. At that point, it was either wait it out until everyone left the house or proceed with the plan. And my judgment at that time, and any judgment can be questioned, was that we should, in fact, proceed with the plan."

Sambor answered Kauffman by assigning responsibility to one of his subordinates when he said, "Captain Shanahan, to whom the order was given, was well aware of the importance of it, because we discussed the importance, the potential danger to the children on many an occasion. And this was one of the things that we were most concerned about."

There is a logical link between the failure to pick up the children and the decision not to stop the operation on May 13, and rethink the plan. More time would have provided more opportunities to remove the children from danger. More time would have allowed for scrutiny of the plan to drop the bomb and the development of alternatives to the bomb. Another day or two, or even a week, could have provided better opportunities and options than those available to the Big Four as evening settled on Osage Avenue and they pushed to end the confrontation that day.

Brooks had his sharpest disagreement with the mayor and Sambor about the decision to complete the operation before nightfall. If there was an issue which fractured the Big Four collegium it was their recollection of how they responded to the most logical alternative available to them on May 13. The logic of waiting and reconsidering was reinforced by State Senator Hardy Williams' telephone call to the mayor in the afternoon, suggesting that the city suspend and reconsider the operation, and my call to the mayor in the morning, advising him to withdraw the police because they were not trained for the situation which confronted them. Fire commissioner Richmond was not directly involved in the decision, but his concern about the safety of firefighters provided an additional reason why any operation after dark would have caused him special problems.

Brooks, Sambor and the mayor each had been questioned about the decision not to suspend the operation after it was apparent their plan had failed. The mayor testified, on the morning of October 15, that he was prepared to suspend the operation and wait as long as it took, if that had been recommended by Brooks and Sambor. The mayor focused responsibility for the tactics on Sambor under the supervision of Brooks. The mayor was asked, "Did you leave the question of whether or not there should be a deadline up to commissioner Sambor or Mr. Brooks or anyone else?"

He answered, "The entire tactical plan was to be planned and executed by the police commissioner under the supervision of the managing director, with the mayor being kept informed each step of the way in terms of what they were doing. And my instruction was, 'I don't mean to hear about it on television first. I want to know about it before it appears on television.'"

The next day, October 16, Brooks had a different recollection about suspending the operation and who was involved in deciding to continue despite their failures. Contrary to the mayor's assertion that there was no expressed concern about the need to complete the operation on May 13, Brooks testified it was an issue which he discussed "at great length" with Sambor and "at least once or twice with the mayor during that evening."

According to Brooks, the logic of suspending the operation was overruled by four tactical considerations: the desire of the residents who had been evacuated to return to their homes that day, the approach of evening and the possibility that the people in the MOVE house might escape from the house, fear that MOVE combatants would use tunnels to enter other houses on the block, and concern that the police officers had been on duty too long and were getting tired.

The reasons given by Brooks for pushing to complete the operation were plausible, but they were insignificant when compared to the danger to the children in the house. Nevertheless Brooks was certain the option of suspending the operation had been considered and rejected.

Q. Who made the decision not to wait and regroup and see what could be done the next day?

A. I don't think there was a decision that was made not to wait and regroup. I think the decision was it is better to continue.

Q. And who made that decision?

A. Oh I think, I think that was an evolution, the commissioner made that recommendation to me more than once. And I discussed that at least once or twice with the mayor during the evening.

Q. Would it be fair to say that was the decision that was made both—not just both but by the commissioner of police, yourself and the mayor?

A. I think that's fair to say.

Two days later Sambor denied he had a discussion with Brooks about the necessity to complete the operation before nightfall, or for any other reason. Sambor said Brooks was mistaken. Sambor claimed they did not end the operation when their plan failed because there were a few hours of daylight remaining, and using the bomb to blow a hole in the roof would place them in a better position on the following day.

Commissioners Bronson, Lillie and Kauffman focused their questions to the mayor, Sambor and Brooks on why they did not accept the logic of suspending the operation and rethinking their plans. Lillie asked them if they gave any consideration to "just doing nothing, just allowing the tempest to cool and perhaps letting this go over into the second day."

Bronson asked if there was a tacit understanding or pervasive feeling that the operation had to be completed that day. Kauffman was incredulous when he asked why the mayor did not end the operation by the afternoon of May 13, because by then he knew the experts he relied on had failed.

Brooks' recollection was irreconcilable with the testimony of the mayor and Sambor. Each of them answered without a glance toward the colleague whom they contradicted. They seemed to stiffen in their chairs, they leaned forward, their arms on the table before them, and they spoke slowly and purposefully. They were, for the first time during the hearings, drawing lines that separated them and defined their credibility.

Brooks flatly contended that Sambor had led him to believe "that we would lose so much control during the night and that the other community pressures and et cetera, when you put all that together, that he had to go on and I recall it from a conversation at some point in the afternoon when he says I prayed to the Lord, or something to that effect, that you do work out a way to use the crane because if you don't, we are going to have to do something more drastic." They did do something more drastic, they dropped the bomb. The bomb was too drastic a step not to have been conceived under pressure of a deadline. The bomb was too risky if there was no opposition to continuing the next day. More importantly, the deadline defined the true purpose of the bomb. The bomb was intended to end the operation, to finish it once and for all.

Sambor contradicted Brooks on the deadline, because the deadline gave the bomb more terrible dimensions and implications. As police commissioner, Sambor had to be aware of the criminal implications of dropping a bomb to end the operation as compared to his claim that the purpose of the bomb was to cut a hole in the roof of the house and also to move the bunker from the roof.

The mayor's failure to lead the operation at the scene had its greatest effect on the decision to push on with the bomb because he did not hear the discussion Brooks heard, and more importantly, he did not observe the desperation inherent in Sambor's statement that he prayed for the crane as an alternative to the drastic action he was considering. Had the mayor fully understood Sambor's attitude, he would have known the bomb was more than a device to cut a hole in the roof.

The mayor was in his office. The battle was no more than flickering pictures on his television. He was too remote from the action to make the critical decisions he made, and he acknowledged that in answer to a question from Kauffman when he said, "You're asking me to go back and unmake a decision which I've made. I made that decision and I'm here today because I made that decision and you're here today because I made that decision. And this whole inquiry is taking place because I made that decision."

GAS AND BULLETS

Tear gas and Bullets are weapons and, depending on the circumstances, each is capable of inflicting serious injury and death. Moreover, some types of tear gas are more powerful and therefore more deadly than others. Sambor and Brooks claimed that the reliance on tear gas as the basic weapon of their plan was an indication of their concern for the children and the innocent adults in the MOVE house. However, they did not know what type tear gas the police used until after the confrontation.

The police had two types of tear gas available to them, "CN gas" and "CS gas." According to the Smith & Wesson weapons catalogue, CN gas is safe and effective when used by trained personnel. CS gas is described in the catalogue as stronger than CN gas. CS was developed by the United States Army for outdoor use. It is utilized best in grenades and projectiles, and it causes severe stinging in the eyes and the feeling of suffocation.

Ordinarily CS gas would not be lethal if used outdoors because it is diluted and dissipated by the air, and victims can escape to fresh air. Injecting CS gas into an enclosed area intensifies its effect. Therefore, if CS gas was injected into the MOVE house, the implication of malice is clear. It is an implication which attaches to the leadership of the Big Four because it was their responsibility to know and understand the character and the extent of the weaponry the police planned to use.

Since the mayor did not evaluate or review the plans for the assault, he had no knowledge or interest in the potency of the tear gas police planners intended to use. Richmond and Sambor attended meetings where the plan was reviewed and the types of tear gas were mentioned, but neither of them asked any questions about the types of gas to be used and their effect on the children and other residents of the house. Sambor knew there were differences between CN and CS gases. He knew that one lasted longer than the other and was more debilitating than the other, but he

did not know which was which. He also did not know which gas
was actually used by police under his command on May 13 until
he read a report after that date. It was then he learned that CS gas
was used.

While some confusion about the character and use of tear
gas may be understandable, there is no excuse for the dangerous
confusion among the Big Four about the firearms that were used.
When Mayor Goode testified individually on October 15, 1985, he
said he received a briefing from Sambor on May 11, 1985, and at
that time Sambor told him police would not shoot bullets into the
house but would fire their weapons to give the impression they
were shooting into the house while they waited for the tear gas to
work. Two days later Sambor testified that he never told anyone
police would not shoot into the house.

The mayor also testified that during a telephone call with
Brooks on the morning of May 13, Brooks told him the police were
firing above the house. Brooks testified that he was surprised by
a news report he heard on television about police firing above the
house, and he later told the mayor he had not said police were
firing above the house.

When the Big Four testified, Sambor and Brooks remained
certain they had not said the police fired above the house, and the
mayor said he might have been confused. If the police were
shooting bullets into a house in which there were children, the
mayor should have known about it. His claim of concern for the
welfare of the children must be measured by the extent of his effort
to know the dangers they faced. He did not know, and he did not
make an effort to know.

Brooks and Sambor were certain bullets were fired into the
house. They knew children were somewhere in the house. They
knew bullets entering the house would kill or injure any target they
struck. They knew the children were possible targets. No matter
what the provocation for shooting into the house might have been,
Sambor and Brooks, who were leading the assault, displayed a
reckless disregard for the lives of the children. Pennsylvania law
requires a finding of malice sufficient to support a charge of murder
where a person acts with reckless disregard for causing serious
bodily injury or death to another.

The probability of serious bodily harm or death to occupants
of the MOVE house was increased by the power of the firearms.
The police borrowed heavy weapons—an M-60, three Browning
automatic rifles, a .50-caliber automatic rifle and an anti-tank

gun—from a gun dealer to increase their fire-power. The anti-tank gun was not fired, but the power of the other weapons was enough to show either a reckless disregard for the lives of innocent adults and children within the house or a specific intent to inflict as much bodily harm as possible on everyone within the house.

EXPLOSIVES

The explosives in the bomb created the raging inferno and the central drama of May 13, 1985, and they exposed the existence of a presumption that local police departments have the right to use high explosives against the lives and property of citizens, restrained only by their discretion and judgment.

Except to cause random destruction, Explosives are not trustworthy as weapons and are inappropriate for police actions in densely populated urban neighborhoods. Experts who use Explosives as tools require controlled and stable circumstances to guarantee safety. Sambor insured the use of explosives as a central element of the assault when he ordered the police Bomb Disposal Unit to develop the tactical plan. As a result, before the bomb was dropped, explosives were used in a failed attempt to pierce the party wall to the MOVE house. Explosives were used to explode a party wall to attack suspected MOVE gunmen on the other side of the wall. When the wall was exploded, no one hesitated. No one expressed concern that the explosion might harm or kill children who could have been on the other side of the wall. The police believed they were receiving gunfire through the wall, and they obtained the permission of their superiors to use explosives to blow out the other side of the wall to attack the suspected gunmen.

They had the explosives, they thought they knew how to use them, and they thought their use was justified. It was a simple decision, easily made, and there is nothing to prevent the same decision by local police in almost every jurisdiction.

The police had at least four different high explosives available to them. They were:

1. Tovex—a commercial explosive primarily used in mining operations.
2. HDP—a booster to detonate less sensitive explosives. In civilian use it contains Pentolite, and in military use it contains Tetril.

3. Water gel—a commercial explosive generally containing
   monomethylene nitrates, sodium nitrates and ammonium
   nitrates.
4. C-4—a military plastic explosive which detonates at the rate
   of between 24,000 and 25,000 feet per second. It is three
   times more powerful than dynamite, which detonates at the
   rate of about 8000 feet per second.

Sambor, Brooks and Mayor Goode could not reconcile their
testimony with that of police commanders about their knowledge
of the use of explosives as part of the May 13 plan. Testifying
individually on October 17, Sambor said he did not know, until
after May 13 that Explosives were used to explode the party wall.
Captain Kirshner, Lt. Marandola, and Sgt. Connor contradicted
Sambor. Connor was certain that Sambor was present at a meeting
at 4 A.M. on May 13, when the use of hatch charges to explode the
wall was discussed, and he thought Sambor might have been
present when the same option was discussed on May 11 at a
meeting in Sambor's office. Kirshner and Marandola were certain
that during the operation Sambor participated in a decision to
permit police to explode a hole downward in a party wall to create
a chute for delivering gas into the MOVE house.

When Sambor and Brooks testified jointly with the mayor,
each of them recalled at least one instance when they told the
mayor that explosives would be used as part of the police operation. The mayor said the word "explosives" was never used in his
discussions with them. According to the mayor, Sambor used the
term "wall charge" in discussing the plan, and he thought that
meant the police intended to use an electrical charge.

In response to Brooks' claim that he told the mayor the police
intended to blow holes in the party wall, the mayor said Brooks
used the term "put holes" in the wall, and he thought that meant
they would create the holes mechanically. When asked if he
specifically used the word "explosives" when he discussed the plan
with the mayor, Brooks answered: "I believe I did. If I didn't use
the word explosive, I used the word 'shape charge.' If I didn't use
the word 'shape charge,' I used the expression 'blow a hole' . . . ."

Semantics was the blanket which covered their responsibility
as leaders. The mayor and Sambor indicated they knew so little
about explosives they would not have objected to their use, even
when the usage included the powerful military explosive C-4. Each
of the Big Four ignored their legal, human and moral duties to ask

questions. Human decency required them to try to understand the extent of the danger of using explosives. Once they breached their moral responsibilities by permitting the operation to begin before the children were removed from the house, their only hope for redemption was to proceed so carefully that the safety of the children would be guaranteed.

Their moral duty of care required them to demand detailed explanations and reliable assurances about the likelihood of injury to the children. Their legal duty of care required that they not evidence a reckless disregard for the safety of the children and the innocent adults. Confronted with the significance of their failures, they covered themselves with a blanket of semantics. None of the commissioners believed them. Considering the circumstances we could not believe they could be so callous or so stupid. We could not believe them because we wanted them to be more than they were.

THE BOMB

On May 13, when it was conceived, made and dropped from a helicopter, no one called it a bomb. The men in charge referred to the bomb as a "device." It was a device with a 45-second fuse and several pounds of explosives. It was their intention to explode the device on the roof of the house. None of them thought it was a bomb. In the shattering aftermath of the tragedy they called it an "explosive device." If there is a distinction between their "explosive device" and a bomb, that distinction is far from clear.

Their consideration of the idea to use explosives to dislodge the bunker from the roof of the house was typically shallow, legally culpable and morally reprehensible. Sambor and Police Lt. Powell began preparing to build the bomb at about 3:30 P.M. It was dropped on the house at about 5:20 P.M. In less than two hours the Big Four made the decision to drop explosives on a row house in a densely populated neighborhood.

Everyone involved in making the decision knew the explosives would be dropped from a helicopter except the mayor. He claimed no one told him how the explosives would be delivered to the roof. He didn't ask anyone how the explosives would be delivered, but he claimed that he assumed they would be placed on the roof. The mayor admitted understanding the problem which made the explosives on the roof necessary. He knew the bunker was the insurmountable obstacle which stymied the operation. He knew the decision to try explosives was an alternative to using a crane to remove the bunker from the roof. Based on what he knew, his claim that he believed the explosives would be placed on the roof is incredible. If the position of the bunker prevented police from assaulting the house at ground level, it was a greater deterrent to anyone approaching the house from the roof.

When he was asked if he would have authorized dropping the explosives from a helicopter if he had been told about it, the mayor answered: "if he [Sambor] had called me and told me that in fact he was going to deliver, which is the word he used, an entry device to the roof by helicopter because of the safety of the personnel involved, I do not feel that I would have in fact vetoed that."

Commissioner Ruth's frustration was evident when he challenged the mayor's answer: "But the idea of dropping a bomb, I mean, it would seem that some one of the four people would come here and say, even at the time, even with what we knew or didn't know, it was a bad idea."

The mayor responded to Ruth by relying once more on semantics. He said that he would have rejected the idea if someone had told him they intended to drop a bomb on a row house. He had enough information to reach that conclusion without being told. He had the responsibility to demand specifics from his subordinates that would have fully explained their intentions. Brooks, his driver, Officer Louis Mount, and Sambor contradicted the mayor. They confirmed Brooks' testimony that he told the mayor the explosives would be dropped onto the house from a helicopter.

The mayor steadfastly contended that he was told the "entry device" would be "delivered" to the roof. Since he conceded he would not have vetoed the plan to drop the "device" from a helicopter, the mayor had no objection to dropping an explosive device onto the roof of a row house. Fire commissioner Richmond should have had strenuous objections, or, at least, he should have asked detailed questions to determine the likelihood of fire from the explosives. Instead he relied on the representation of Police Lt. Powell that the explosives were not incendiary in nature and would not cause a fire. Richmond accepted Powell's representation without asking if Powell had ever actually used the explosives or tested them. Richmond did not ask if there were flammable materials on the roof. He did not ask how much heat would be generated by the explosion. He did not discuss what the firefighters would do or could do if the explosion started a fire.

Sambor recalled a discussion by Powell of the type and quantity of explosive in the "entry device" and some mention of testing that determined there was almost no chance of a fire from the explosion. Sambor said the discussion was to allay any concerns Brooks had about safety. Brooks said he never heard the discussion intended for him. Richmond said the same.

The Big Four did not know what was to be dropped on the house because they did not ask. They did not ask because of an assumption of competence. The mayor assumed his commanders at the scene knew what they were doing. Brooks assumed the police knew what they were doing. Richmond assumed Powell knew whether the explosives would start a fire. Sambor assumed Powell knew how to make and drop explosives onto the roof of a house. If any one of the Big Four had asked a few questions, they would have learned their assumptions were wrong.

LETTING THE BUNKER BURN

Justice Kauffman asked the question which went to the central atrocity of the tragedy. "The other area which continues to really gnaw at me is the whole question of the fire, the decision to let the fire burn. Isn't it true, commissioner Sambor and Fire Commissioner Richmond, that you, in effect, made a decision to use the fire as a weapon in this instance?" he asked.

Sambor answered first, "Absolutely not."

"Well you made a decision to let that fire burn until the bunker was destroyed, isn't that right?"

Sambor said that using the fire against people in the house was never a consideration, therefore the fire was not used as a weapon.

Kauffman asked Richmond what he understood Sambor was asking him to do when he asked if they could let the bunker burn. Richmond said there was no one he knew in city government who would intentionally burn people to death. Kauffman retorted that Sambor and Richmond had intentionally risked lives by making a conscious decision to let the fire burn, and they knew what they were doing. Once more Richmond labeled his decision to let the bunker burn a judgment call which required him to balance risks to the lives of firefighters and police against the risk to the children and adults in the house. The imbalance of his judgment was obvious. If he was concerned about gunmen in the bunker wounding or killing city personnel, that danger could not be eliminated by letting the bunker burn. The fire would merely drive the gunmen from the bunker to another position within the house, and the danger to firefighters would remain if they tried to extinguish the fire after the bunker was destroyed. Therefore a decision to let the bunker burn was a decision to let the entire house burn.

Commissioner Ruth questioned Richmond on the details of his thinking. He asked him if he agreed with the testimony of the expert hired by the commission who said that once the bunker burned and fell into the second floor it was inevitable that the entire street would burn down unless the fire could be fought from in front of the house. He wanted to know what was in Richmond's mind as he sat agreeing to let the bunker burn. Had he thought about how long they would let it burn? Richmond said that he agreed with the commission's expert and that he had not thought about how long he would let the bunker burn. He agreed to let it burn until it was no longer usable, but he did not have a clear notion of when that was. In response to further questions about his thinking at the time, he said he thought there was "a possibility and a probability, a degree of both" that he could let the bunker burn and extinguish the fire before the house was destroyed.

He was the expert on the scene, and he realized that he was giving Sambor his expert opinion when he agreed not to fight the fire. An opinion based on both a possibility and a probability that the fire might be extinguished later was not expert. Not only was the decision of Sambor and Richmond inexpert, it also was insubordinate. The fire was a new and unexpected element. Brooks had agreed to the bomb and had recommended it to the mayor after receiving assurances that there was little or no chance of a fire. If Brooks and the mayor had been told there was a significant chance of a fire they might not have approved the bomb. Sambor and Richmond were clearly beyond the scope of the authority granted to them by Brooks and the mayor when they calmly discussed letting the bunker burn. That they did not recognize that limitation, and made no effort to confer with Brooks or the mayor about their scheme to burn the bunker, reveals a callous disregard of their superiors.

Perhaps they were uninhibited because their superiors had not properly asserted their authority throughout the planning and preparation of the operation. Perhaps they were uninhibited because they did not believe their superiors were capable of making the best decision. Whatever the circumstance of their thinking, their actions demonstrated a complete failure of the mayor's leadership. They had not been properly impressed with his authority.

When Brooks realized the danger, he ordered Sambor to, "Put the fire out." Sambor claimed the order was given after Richmond agreed to let the bunker burn, and that Richmond was present and heard the order on the police radio. Richmond vehemently denied that. He claimed he would have obeyed an order by Brooks or the mayor to put the fire out. Sambor and Richmond never sought Brooks' or the mayor's sanction of the decision to let the fire burn, and if they needed to be ordered to put the fire out, the extent of their disdain for their superiors was too great to be overcome.

When their joint testimony ended, the Big Four Finale revealed another tragedy for the city. Philadelphia's first black mayor had placed non-black city officials in a black neighborhood to conduct a hazardous operation, and he could not direct or influence their actions. The hostile spectators who were horrified by an atrocity defined in racial dimensions, and who screamed invectives at the firefighters who did not fight the fire, were partially right. John Africa was partially right. All of the militantly rebellious black leaders since the slave, Nat Turner, were partially right. It was not possible for the established processes of government to accept and respect the meaningful participation and authority of black leadership.

12

THE REPORT

The end of the hearings was a relief. The commissioners returned to their normal schedules. They let distressing details of the tragedy fade a little as they recoiled from daily reviews of witness transcripts, investigation reports and staff memorandums. They could examine emotions which brought some of them to the brink of tears as they inquired into the callousness inherent in the tragedy.

For a few days I tried to re-establish my normal schedule, but I could not. Everything I thought about was colored or interrupted by memories of the testimony. I imagined the agony of innocent children dying alone and frightened. Whether they were killed by police bullets in the alley, or slowly suffocated and burned within the MOVE house, they were executed by their local government. Since the danger to their lives was easily foreseeable, their deaths were legally and morally intentional.

I felt exhausted, but I could not rest. The volumes of testimony and reports, stacked in my den, were irresistible. Each night I reviewed them and categorized them. Somewhere, amid their pages, was the relief I needed. They would help me express what I could not understand. They would help me understand what I needed to express. I could not wait for the commission to write its report. I had to expiate my guilt as a member of the community where an atrocity against children remained unpunished, my guilt as a friend and ally of the mayor who failed to prevent the atrocity.

The commission planned to publish a report in four parts:

A Chronology;
Findings and Conclusions;

158

Recommendations;
Analysis of Evidence;

My discussions with other commissioners indicated an am-
bivalence about how far the report should go in suggesting criminal indictments. We had negotiated the terms of the mayor's
executive order establishing the commission, and paragraph nine
of the order read, "The commission is investigatory only . . . ." In
his letter appointing the commissioners the mayor wrote, "The
public wants the *truth!*" He underlined the word truth. Establishing the truth required more than investigation. An investigation
determines facts. The truth is revealed by weighing and analyzing
facts. Truth requires a judgment and action on that judgment.
That action is justice.

My review of the testimony and other evidence compelled me
to make the judgment that criminal indictments of Sambor and
Richmond were essential to justice. That was the truth I wanted
my report to reveal. That was the truth I wanted the commission's
report to endorse.

Criminal indictments are based on objective consideration of
incriminating facts. Moral infractions and emotional revulsion
cannot substitute for facts which conform to criminal definitions.
The basic elements of every crime are criminal intent and an overt
act. Criminal intent can be a patently evil purpose or such a
reckless disregard for circumstances that an evil purpose will be
presumed. A person who fires a gun in a crowded room may not
intend to wound an innocent bystander, but shooting a gun under
those circumstances demonstrates such a reckless disregard for
the circumstances that criminal intent is presumed.

The mayor's role as a perpetrator of the tragedy had to be
determined by what he knew and by what he did. His poor
leadership and abdication of authority were not enough to establish criminal intent. Based on his testimony, and the testimony of
others who contradicted him but who were more believable, there
were fourteen critical facts which the mayor knew. They were:

1. In late April or early May he was informed about the bunker
   on the roof of the MOVE house.
2. He knew the police had Osage Avenue under 24-hour
   surveillance.

3. By May 1, 1985, he knew there might be explosives in the MOVE house and that there might have been tunnels under Osage Avenue.
4. He was told of a plan to pick up the children before the police operation.
5. He knew the children might be used as hostages.
6. He knew MOVE was prepared for a confrontation with police.
7. He knew the police commissioner prepared the plan and the date of the operation was May 13.
8. He knew the plan involved using tear gas, water and a "stun-gun" to dislodge the residents of the MOVE house.
9. He knew the police did not pick up the children before the operation began.
10. He knew there was gasoline on the roof of the MOVE house.
11. By the afternoon of May 13, he knew police had fired automatic weapons at the MOVE house and not above the house.
12. He knew the tear gas and water did not work.
13. He knew a helicffopter would be used to drop explosives on the roof of the MOVE house.
14. He knew the MOVE house was on fire and firefighters were not fighting the fire.

If the mayor had properly analyzed what he knew, he would have foreseen the disastrous results of the flawed plan. His failure to analyze the facts properly and to give more consideration to the substance of the operation was grossly negligent and pitifully inept. He abdicated his authority. He relinquished his leadership. He abandoned the children to the expediencies of the police and fire commissioners. He should have known more about what they were doing and why they were doing it. He knew enough to provide better leadership, but he did not know enough to demonstrate a reckless disregard for the circumstances.

It would have been easier to obtain indictments of Richmond and Sambor if there was a basis for indicting the mayor. A thin wall of ignorance protected him from the criminal consequences of his failures. The same wall of ignorance also protected Brooks. There was no protection for Sambor and Richmond. They alone decided to let the bunker burn; Goode and Brooks were not parties to their conspiracy. They alone knew they were exposing the lives of the children to the unpredictably hazardous circumstances of fire.

Their reckless disregard for the lives of the children and adults in the house was inescapable. Their decision distinguished them from Goode and Brooks. They were also distinguished from their superiors by their racial identities. As I worked on my report I knew Sambor and Richmond would not be held to account for their crimes. I knew there was not enough moral fortitude within the legal system to indict two white commanders and absolve two black commanders. It was a sad realization. My hope was in the commission. It could be the instrument of retribution. It could demand the indictment of Richmond and Sambor. It could demand Richmond's dismissal. If the commission would not condemn them, my report would accuse them. I wrote:

I do not believe the absence of a direct order to put the fireout, or the suggestion of Sambor to let the fire burn justifies Richmond's failure to immediately fight the fire. As the fire commissioner he should have rejected the tactical use of fire no matter who wanted to do it.

As Police Commissioner Sambor violated what was reasonable and prudent conduct by a police officer in seeking to use fire as a tactical weapon on a building which housed innocent children. Since there is no dispute about the conclusion that prior to 6:15 P.M. the fire was an incipient fire which could have been easily extinguished by the squirt guns without exposing firemen to the threat of gunfire, I believe the decision to let the fire burn was the primary cause of the death and destruction of May 13.

It is my opinion that Fire Commissioner Richmond disregarded his lawful duty and demonstrated a disregard for human life and an indifference to the consequences to the children and adults occupying 6221, in an effort to assist and abet Sambor whose primary concern was the destruction of the bunker. It is my opinion that Sambor knowingly disobeyed the orders of the mayor and the managing director when he knew or should have known they were directing him to preserve life and property, and when he knew or should have known that his disobedience, under those circumstances constituted reckless disregard of the consequences, regardless of his official duty, and indicated an unjustified disregard for the probability of death or great bodily harm, and extreme indifference to the value of human life.

I worked on my report throughout November and December. When the commission began its deliberations, the first draft of my report was completed. H. Graham McDonald, deputy staff director, to the commission, visited me in early January to discuss how the deliberations would proceed. The commission's staff met with each commissioner and prepared 22 proposed findings based on those meetings. The proposed findings were to be the starting point of the deliberations.

I gave the staff a copy of my report, and I also submitted proposed findings. The outcome of the commission's deliberations was expressed in its report, Kauffman's dissents from sections of the report, and in my report. The route to that outcome required each commissioner to become totally immersed in the issues and emotions of the judgments which were made and the tough compromises which were necessary.

The commission's report represented unanimous agreement on 66 of 68 findings, conclusions and recommendations. The report contained 31 specific findings of fact and conclusions related to twelve aspects of the tragedy. The first two findings described the hostility of the MOVE organization in the 1980's.

Findings 3 through 9 described the mayor's policy of appeasement of MOVE and the impact of that policy on the deteriorating situation on Osage Avenue.

Findings 10 through 13 delineated the flaws and failures of police planning of the May 13 operation.

Findings 14 through 16 and 29 described the disregard for the safety of the children.

Findings 17 and 22 established the mayor's abdication of his authority.

Findings 18 through 20 concluded that the force used by police during the attack on the MOVE house was excessive and unconscionable.

Finding 21 described the involvement of the Federal Bureau of Investigation with the bomb. An FBI agent gave the police Bomb Disposal Unit the powerful military explosive C-4 which was used in the bomb.

Finding 23 described the defective communications during the operation.

Findings 24 through 27 established facts and conclusions regarding the bomb and the fire.

Finding 28 concluded that police gunfire in the rear alley prevented the escape from the fire of some occupants of the MOVE house.

Finding 30 established that six adults were killed.

Finding 31 concluded that the city medical examiner performed unprofessionally and in violation of generally accepted practices for pathologists.

The deliberations began with a consensus that the children were victims of an atrocity and the Big Four were primarily responsible for the fatally flawed operation. There was never a suggestion that any of the commanders acted properly and were faultless. That initial consensus helped to keep the debate civil and relevant. As to the leaders, our differences were about the extent and quality of their guilt.

Six of the eleven commissioners were lawyers. Lawyers use language in a jurisprudential context which often eludes non-lawyers. Terms such as "gross negligence" have legal definitions of civil and criminal liability. The non-lawyer commissioners were concerned that they would agree to language which the lawyers understood as a commitment to a legal position the non-lawyers did not intend.

That problem was resolved during the first meeting of the deliberations. It was agreed that the words used in the report would be used in their normal, non-legal context. The first meeting of the deliberations began at 10 A.M., Saturday, January 18, 1986. We had been a commission for eight months. They were eight months of intensive work. None of us knew each other as well before we began our work as we did on January 18. All of the commissioners were prepared to begin considering the proposed findings. They had clear recollections of the testimony and other evidence, and they had positions on the evidence.

There were six black members and five white members, but there was never a racial split in the deliberations. They knew their judgments would have a profound impact on the lives of the participants in the tragedy and on the Philadelphia electorate. They could not restore the lives which were lost. They could not end or soothe the anguish of the survivors. They were an instrument for abstract justice—a preacher's justice of chastening words and troubling revelations. They were determined to fulfill their mission. As they discussed and debated, it was obvious that their

pronouncement of judgment would be direct, specific and damning. Reaching agreement on the language of their pronouncement
and the scope of its condemnations was not easy.

Drafting their findings proceeded by a system of colored
sheets of paper. The first draft of a proposed finding was submitted
on white paper. Revisions of the finding were on green paper, and
the final version of the finding was on blue paper.

Final versions were also subject to further consideration and
revision. Some of the final versions were divided into subsections
such as 14-A, 14-B and 14-C, which were numbered in the report,
14, 15 and 16.

The commissioners sat for hours, poring over the colored
sheets, wrestling with the words, as they tried to define their
positions precisely. They were congenial, sometimes jovial, through
the dark, cold winter evenings and Saturdays, but a confrontation
was inevitable. There were two irreconcilable positions on the
responsibility of police officers. Kauffman was determined that no
fault should be ascribed to them. He was prepared to condemn the
police commissioner, but he would not allow any criticism of the
officers.

There were commissioners who were willing to try to accommodate Kauffman's position to achieve a unanimous report. The
commission chairman and I were among those commissioners
who were not willing to accommodate Kauffman. As the commission considered each proposed finding, it bypassed those where
there was serious disagreement. They would be revisited after
agreement on the others. Findings 1 to 13 were agreed to by
February 11, 1986. Findings 14 to 16 dealt with the children and
were more difficult to resolve.

The proposed finding submitted by the staff as number 12
but which became number 14 during green-sheet revisions and
number 15 in the report, read:

> The mayor's failure to call a halt to the operation, when,on May 13th
> he knew that the MOVE Children were in the house and that no
> effort had been made to remove them, was grossly negligent and
> displayed a callous indifference to the lives of those children.

All of the initial proposals were written by Emerson Moran,
the communications officer. He had been selected to handle the
news media and to write the report. The commissioners immediately agreed with what Moran was trying to express, but they

doubted the necessity of saying the mayor was "grossly negligent" and that he "displayed a callous indifference to the lives of those children."

Henry Ruth said that gross negligence was callous indifference and that it wasn't necessary to use both terms in the finding. Reverend Bronson said there had to be some statement of how the mayor's negligence affected the lives of the children. I agreed with her and said we could use both terms for emphasis. Kauffman provided the answer. He said the mayor had risked the lives of the children and we had to say that. Todd Cooke suggested the language which everyone accepted. He read from his notes, "was grossly negligent and clearly risked the lives of those children."

Thus the final version was:

The mayor's failure to call a halt to the operation on May 13th, when he knew that the children were in the house, was grossly negligent and clearly risked the lives of those children.

Proposed finding 17 was a single sentence:

The gunfire brought to bear by the police against the MOVE house was excessive and unconscionable.

The last word of the sentence ignited the only angry debate of the deliberations. Kauffman would not accept the accusation that police officers acted unconscionably. He argued that once police were fired upon they had a right to shoot back with everything they had. "What about the children?" I asked.

He responded that rank-and-file police officers were not responsible for the situation. If there was any unconscionable act it was with the mayor and the other leaders who placed police in a situation where they had to defend their lives. Cooke joined Kauffman. He also thought police had a right to shoot back with everything they had. Brown asked them if they thought police had no responsibility to consider the danger to the children and other innocent bystanders. Kauffman said again that the mayor should have thought of that before he placed the police in danger and that there was no evidence that police bullets had harmed anyone.

Father Washington, Reverend Bronson and Lillie each rebutted the notion that police had no responsibility to consider the danger to the children. Ruth added that we were expressing concern about the consciences of the police and not their legal authority to shoot back. Father Washington was eloquent and angry when he said that we could not accept a double standard which permits police officers to ignore the humanity of children in some neighborhoods and not in others. Kauffman was terse when he replied that the neighborhood had nothing to do with it, the police were under attack.

I insisted that the neighborhood did have something to do with it and that I did not believe we should approve of police making war against children. Cooke turned to me and asked, "What would you do if a group of teenagers dragged you into an alley and tried to rob you?"

"I wouldn't try to kill them," I replied.

"Most people would do whatever they could to defend themselves," he said.

Monsignor Cullen calmed the anger when he said they were considering the actions of police as part of a planned operation, and he thought that as a matter of conscience they were obliged to consider the danger to the children, no matter what their legal authority may have been. Kauffman insisted that those considerations were left to the mayor and the other leaders of the operation. Several commissioners tried to write an acceptable compromise. They tried to appease Kauffman by setting forth the circumstances and they wrote:

> The firing of over 10,000 rounds of ammunition, during a 90 minute period, at a row house containing children, was clearly excessive and unconscionable.

Kauffman would not accept it, and revised wording was proposed:

> The firing of over 10,000 rounds of ammunition at a row house containing children, was clearly excessive. The authorization of such an excessive amount of force was unconscionable.

Kauffman's arguments had made an impact. Most of the commissioners were willing to link the authorization of the excessive force to the word unconscionable. Kauffman considered the compromise but decided he could not accept a statement that police force was excessive. Cooke said that he could accept the compromise.

Brown and I were not willing to absolve the individual police officers. No matter what their leaders ordered, they knew children were in the house. They could have refused to shoot their weapons. I reminded the commissioners that the Nuremberg trials established a standard of personal responsibility which no longer permitted subordinates to claim they were following orders when they committed atrocities. The second revision read:

> The firing of over 10,000 rounds of ammunition at a row house containing children, was clearly excessive and unreasonable.The failure to control those officers involved in such an excessive amount of force was unconscionable.

It was a compromise which recognized the excessive police force but assigned responsibility for the unconscionable nature of the force to the commanders who led the police.

Kauffman would not accept it. He said he would dissent from any finding which accused police of using excessive force. Brown was prepared to accept Kauffman's dissent and move on. The compromises had the support of every commissioner except Kauffman. The discussion had evolved a firm determination to brand killing children "unconscionable."

Cooke made another attempt to include Kauffman. Throughout the deliberations Cooke fought hardest for unanimity. No matter how many proposals were rejected, Cooke was willing to try another approach. He listened intently to the objections and reservations of the other commissioners and then drafted new words which they might all embrace. His language was always ingenious, but he was always willing to change it if the change would create a consensus.

During one discussion, after watching him absorb and respond to comments and reservations from almost every commissioner, and each time present new language that sought to accommodate them all, I said softly, "Todd, I don't know how you do it . . . You have the patience of Job." His patience and diplomacy were respected by the commissioners, and, as a result, he convinced them to try once more.

> The firing of over 10,000 rounds of ammunition, in under 90 minutes at a row house was clearly excessive and unreasonable. The failure of those responsible for the firing to control or stop such an excessive amount of force was unconscionable.

Police officers were not named. "Those responsible for the firing" could have been the officers or their superiors. There was no reference to the children, thus uncoupling the excessive police force from the death of the children.

Kauffman hesitated. I thought I saw a fleeting wistful expression on his face which indicated he wanted to find a compromise. He too had said he hoped for a unanimous report, but he raised his chin and said he would have to dissent. Defending his version of the innocence of the police officers was a principle he would not abandon.

The single sentence of the white sheet-proposal numbered 17 which caused the first dissent, was developed into a combination of the best of the compromises, and became finding number 18 in the report:

> The firing of over 10,000 rounds of ammunition, in under 90 minutes at a row house containing children was clearly excessive and unreasonable. The failure of those responsible for the firing to control or stop such an excessive amount of force was unconscionable.

The struggle to prevent dissent had failed. Kauffman would write a response to the finding and dispute the legal basis for accusing the police of excessive force. He would also ridicule the majority which labored to find common ground with him. At the conclusion of his dissent he misrepresented the commission's finding as one based primarily on the number of rounds fired into the house. He wrote:

> The majority simply concludes that 10,000 rounds were too many. While assuming the role of critic, the majority does not state how many rounds of what type of weapons would have been appropriate in the battlefield conditions MOVE had created. Would they have approved 5,000 rounds? 2,000? 500? Where would they, through hindsight, draw that arbitrary line? I refuse to join this criticism which is grossly unfair and unwarranted.

Kauffman knew that the issue for the commission was not the number of rounds fired, it was the danger to the children. The number of rounds fired was fixed by the facts. There was a relationship between the number of times bullets smashed into the house and the probability of harm to the children, but it was the probability of harm to them that motivated the commission's finding. Kauffman had a right to disagree and to dissent, but he did not have the right to betray the sincere deliberations of the commission by ridicule and misrepresentation.

Kauffman dissented again when the commission decided that police gunfire prevented some of the occupants of the burning building from escaping the fire. He also dissented from one of the commission's final comments which opined that racism was involved in the tragedy because:

> . . . the decisions of various city officials to permit construction of the bunker; to allow the use of high explosives, and in a 90 minute period, the firing of at least 10,000 rounds of ammunition at the house; to sanction the dropping of a bomb on an occupied row house; and to let a fire burn in a row house occupied by children, would not likely have been made had the MOVE house and its occupants been situated in a comparable white neighborhood.

As we neared the end of our deliberations, I reminded the commissioners of the first meeting of the commission when I said the black community expected the commission to determine whether racial considerations were factors in the tragedy. Brown quickly said the commission would have to make a decision about that. Kauffman objected. He said there was no evidence of racial considerations since the mayor and managing director were both black. He argued that any mention of race would adversely affect the community.

I stood and leaned forward with my knuckles pressed against the conference table top. I spoke slowly as I tried to disguise the anger I felt. "Goode and Brooks did not shoot ten thousand bullets into that house, they did not put military explosives into the bomb, they did not decide to let the bunker burn, and they did not shoot at children trying to escape the fire. I know none of that would have happened in a white neighborhood and so do you."

Kauffman said he did not believe race was a factor and if we said it was, he would dissent again. I responded that if we did not say race was a factor, I would dissent. Brown said he would join my dissent, as did Lillie and Reverend Bronson. Ruth said that the commission could not avoid the racial implications. Monsignor Cullen said that if we thought there were racial implications to the tragedy, then we had to say so.

Father Washington was troubled by the consideration of race alone. He believed there were racial considerations in the decision-making, but he also thought there were economic ones. He believed poor white children would have been treated with equal callousness. "I think we have to say this would not have happened in a comparable middle class white neighborhood, because I believe it would have happened in a poor white neighborhood," he said.

He made a distinction which everyone, except Kauffman, could accept. There was no serious effort to dissuade Kauffman from a dissent. After the first dissent it did not matter how many times he dissented.

The last meeting of the deliberations began after 5 P.M. on Monday, February 24, 1986. Earlier that month a subcommittee of Cooke, Ruth and myself submitted a draft of "Recommendations" to be included in the report. What the city needed to do was very obvious, and the Recommendations were easily approved. As we rode the elevators to the thirty-sixth floor conference room of Brown's law firm, we knew the weary journey through the findings and conclusions was about to end. We did not know how it would end. There was one remaining issue. We had to decide whether to recommend the dismissal of the fire commissioner, and the resignation of the mayor. Sambor and Brooks had resigned. Goode and Richmond were the only two of the Big Four remaining in office.

Welch and I were certain the fire commissioner should be dismissed. When the fire started his duty was clear. He disregarded his duty. No one disagreed with the removal of Richmond. If he had done his duty the children would have survived. The problem was the mayor.

Cooke began the debate. He thought the commission should not make any comment about the status of Richmond or the mayor. Their status was beyond the scope of the commission's authority. The appealing logic of his argument was that the responsibility to study our findings and demand whatever action was appropriate belonged to the electorate.

I agreed that a commission should not try to instruct voters about their elected officials. There was no rationale for a commission of private citizens demanding the resignation of an elected official. Richmond was not elected. He was appointed by the mayor. He failed the mayor, who had a right to expect him to do his duty. There was every reason to demand Richmond's dismissal. Ruth and Monsignor Cullen argued that seeking Richmond's dismissal without the mayor's resignation would make our group appear to be the "Mayor's commission."

The specter of the early criticism from the news media stood at the center of the debate. Cullen demanded identical treatment of Richmond and Goode. If we demanded Richmond's dismissal, we had to also demand Goode's resignation. He was prepared to ask for both. He believed they were equally guilty of the deaths of the children.

The morality of his position was persuasive. The responsibility imposed by law and the responsibility imposed by conscience could be miles apart, and they could both be right. Cullen was a priest, a man of conscience. He could easily discern the inseparability of Goode and Richmond. As lawyers it was easier for Welch and me to see the distinctions between them. Moreover a recommendation to dismiss Richmond could be enforced by the mayor. Only the voters could remove the mayor.

Father Washington and Reverend Bronson shared Cullen's moral insights. Washington believed the mayor was responsible for the entire tragedy, and Bronson objected to trying merely to finesse the issue. The debate had reached a point where fact, morality and truth would not congeal. The unlimited scope of moral precepts could link everyone aware of the operation in a chain of responsibility, but that would not be truthful. Without discrediting moral responsibility, truth focuses on personal liability. It is the assessment of liability which makes justice possible. Richmond was personally liable as well as morally responsible, and it was not true that his personal liability could not be separated from Goode's moral responsibility.

A clear statement about Richmond's liability was the only hope of justice for the dead children. Justice required a demand for his dismissal and indictment as partial payment of his unsatisfied debt to the dead children.

At the start of the deliberations I submitted proposed findings which included:

The joint decision of Police Commissioner Gregore Sambor and Fire Commissioner William Richmond to let the bunker burn was the direct and most immediate cause of the death and destruction which occurred on May 13 on Osage Avenue and appropriate legal action should be instituted against them.

The mayor had not done anything that came close to the evilness of the decision to let the bunker burn. Ruth, Bronson, Cooke and Cullen insisted that the mayor and Richmond were inextricably linked. Welch, Lillie, Kauffman, Washington, Mrs. Chinn, and I thought Richmond should be dismissed. Brown did not take a position, except that he was not willing to accept a four-to-six vote. He pushed the debate along, hoping for a compromise.

It came from Washington. He maintained that it wasn't necessary to spell out what should happen to Richmond and the mayor because the report speaks for itself. I did not believe that was true. The report of findings and conclusions did not demand Richmond's dismissal. It did not establish his culpability for the dead children.

The evening meeting had lasted into night. Lights of office buildings spangled the darkness outside the wide windows of the conference room. It was getting colder outside as the hours passed. I knew the commissioners had enough. It was not Cullen's clear moral challenge or my distinctions which decided the last issue in the report. It was human fatigue. It was the natural limit on the best people have to give. It was the desire to get out of that room, through the cold, dark night and home. I made it unanimous. We wrote that the report spoke for itself.

Ahead of the commission was the press conference to release the report, controversies about leaked copies of the report, and a staff memo which was withheld from the commissioners. The memo was a law student's analysis which contradicted the time when the mayor said he ordered Brooks to "put the fire out." The memorandum was not important because Brooks, Richmond and Sambor did not need an order from the mayor to know they should fight a fire.

The night was cold when I left the building. I was proud of my report because it said what the commission's report did not say. It would be published along with the commission's findings. It accused Richmond and Sambor of the crime of letting the bunker burn. An accusation wasn't justice, but it was better than no accusation at all.

Something I learned in high school buoyed my spirits. I was taught that "truth crushed to earth will rise again." "It will," I thought, "sooner or later, it will."

EPILOGUE

Recommendation number twenty-nine of the Commission Report was unanimously approved by the commissioners. It said:

29. Five children were killed during the confrontation on May 13, 1985. Their deaths appear to be unjustified homicides which should be investigated by a grand jury.

The homicides of the children were investigated by two grand juries. A state grand jury, impaneled by Philadelphia District Attorney Ronald Castille and a federal grand jury impaneled by the U.S. Department of Justice. Castille was elected district attorney a few days prior to the end of the commission's public hearings. Castille also presented evidence related to the May 13, 1985 tragedy to two state indicting grand juries.

One grand jury indicted Ramona Africa, (Ramona Johnson), the only adult victim of the tragedy to escape alive, on the following charges: criminal conspiracy, possession of an instrument of crime generally, possession of an instrument of crime, a weapon, simple assault, aggravated assault, reckless endangering another person, riot, and resisting arrest. Mayor Goode and Police Commissioner Sambor were among the witnesses who testified for the prosecution at her trial. She was convicted and sentenced to prison.

Castille's other grand jury indicted the black contractor who was awarded the contract to rebuild the Osage Avenue neighborhood. He was convicted of misapplying some of the money allocated for the construction.

According to the Department of Justice, the F.B.I. began an investigation of the May 13 tragedy in July of 1975, and the federal

173

grand jury investigation began in April of 1987. On September 20, 1988, Assistant Attorney General William Bradford Reynolds issued a statement that no one would be indicted. Reynolds' three paragraph news release mentioned that the F.B.I. "carefully considered" the statements of over 250 witnesses, but there was no indication of the reasons no one was indicted.

In April 1988, Castille's grand jury, which investigated the tragedy, issued a 279-page report. The report was actually written by Castille's assistants and then approved by the members of the grand jury. It would require another book to analyze the distortions and rationalizations used to justify the report's conclusion that no one who attacked the MOVE house should be indicted. The policy of no indictments was applied to two police officers who, according to the grand jury, committed perjury when they lied during the investigation. Both of the policemen, Officer Klein and Sgt. Connor were members of the police bomb squad. Klein made the bomb that was dropped on the MOVE house.

Castille cloaked Klein and Connor with the protection of his prosecutorial discretion. Klein retired from the police department with a "psychiatric disability." Connor left the Philadelphia Police Department to continue his law enforcement career elsewhere.

It took three years and four months to sweep the homicides of five innocent children under official rugs. The policeman who made the bomb so powerful that a presumption of malice was inescapable, did escape his conduct and his perjury about his conduct. Sambor and Richmond, who ignored the authority of Mayor Goode and Managing Director Brooks, when they decided to let the bunker burn, retired from their positions without penalty. Goode was re-elected mayor by a narrow margin. He defeated former Mayor Frank Rizzo. Novella Williams was one of the leaders of Rizzo's campaign.

In 1988, Bennie Swans was accused of mismanagement of the Crisis Intervention Network and the program was denied further funding by Goode. Police officer Berghaier resigned from the police force. Birdie Africa (Moses Ward) was reunited with his father and introduced to America's middle class lifestyle. Brooks retreated to a general's retirement in Virginia.

After considerable wrangling about everything from the design of the new houses to the warranty on their roofs, the Osage neighborhood was rebuilt and reoccupied. In 1988, Dr. Pernsley resigned as commissioner of the Philadelphia Department of

Human Services after a controversy about the department's failure to protect children from abuse.

The commission concluded its report with a comment on the racial connotations inherent in the tragedy. It wrote:

> Despite the progress which has been made in recent decades toward achieving greater equality, the sad fact exists that racial and other prejudices remain in our society. Black and white leadership accordingly must recognize that the decision-making process, both public and private, may consciously or unconsciously be influenced by race, socioeconomic conditions and the lack of political power. The commission believes that the decisions of various city officials to permit construction of the bunker; to allow the use of high explosives, and in a 90 minute period, the firing of at least 10,000 rounds of ammunition at the house; to sanction the dropping of a bomb on an occupied row house; and to let the fire burn in a row house occupied by children, would not likely have been made had the MOVE house and its occupants been situated in a comparable white neighborhood.

That closing comment was confirmed by the failure of the grand juries to indict anyone except a black woman who was a victim and a black man who misappropriated money. The grand juries expanded the tragedy. In addition to the blood of innocent children and the indelible images of the fire, Philadelphia was permanently stained by a gross miscarriage of justice.

In November 1988, Commission Chairman Brown commented on Castille's grand jury in an interview by The Legal Intelligencer newspaper. Brown said that the Castille grand jury had more than enough evidence to warrant criminal indictments. Brown placed the responsibility for the failure to indict with Castille. According to the interviewer he said, "It's the district attorney who really controls where the grand jury is. If the district attorney indicates to them that there really isn't anything there to indict, the grand jury pretty much accepts that."

If the commission was right in its assessment that there would have been different decisions and a different result if the MOVE house had been situated in a comparable white neighborhood, then perhaps Castille's grand jury would have been convinced to indict the men who let the bunker burn if the dead black children had been comparable white children. One thing is certain. The dead children have been denied justice. Justice denied to anyone is justice destroyed for everyone.

GLOSSARY

Africa, Birdie (Moses Ward). Black male, age 13, the only child to escape the MOVE house alive. He escaped with Ramona. Testified for the commission. His mother, Rhonda Africa, was killed during the confrontation.

Africa, Conrad (James Conrad Hampton). Black male, MOVE leader, age 30-45, determined by the commission pathologist. Listed on one of the arrest warrants. He was leader of MOVE members inside 6221 Osage Avenue.

Africa, Delicia. Child, black female, age 9-12, determined by the commission pathologist. Killed during the confrontation.

Africa, Frank (Frank James). Black male, age 25-35 determined by the commission pathologist. MOVE member listed on arrest warrant. Killed during the confrontation.

Africa, Gerald (Gerald Robert Ford). MOVE Minister of Information. He was not in the Osage Avenue house during the confrontation. He gave a statement to the commission, but he refused to testify.

Africa, John (Vincent Leaphart). Black male, age 50, determined by the commission pathologist. Founder and prophet of the MOVE cult. Killed during the confrontation.

Africa, Katricia (Katricia "Tree" Dotson). Child, black female, age 13-15, determined by the commission pathologist. Her remains included, cut-off blue jeans. Birdie Africa saw her escape the house and run down the rear alley. Killed during the confrontation.

176

Africa, Netta (Zenetta Dotson). Child, black female, age 11-14, determined by the commission pathologist. Her remains included a white shirt with red trim. Killed during the confrontation.

Africa, Phil. Child, black male, age 10-12, determined by the commission pathologist. Birdie Africa saw him escape the burning house and run down the rear alley. Killed during the confrontation.

Africa, Ramona (Ramona Johnson). MOVE member, black female. She was the only adult to escape the MOVE house.

Africa, Raymond (Raymond Foster). MOVE member, adult black male, insufficient remains to determine age. Killed during the confrontation.

Africa, Rhonda (Rhonda Harris). MOVE member, black female, age 25-30, determined by the commission pathologist. Birdie Africa's mother. Killed during the confrontation.

Africa, Theresa (Theresa Brooks). MOVE member, black female, age 18-25, determined by the commission pathologist. Remains were exhumed after cremation and burial. Killed during the confrontation.

Africa, Temasa. Child, black male, age 7-9 determined by the commission pathologist. Killed during the confrontation.

Angelucci, Daniel. Police officer, Bomb Disposal Unit. Refused to testify.

Bariana, Marcus. Police officer assigned to Post four overlooking the alley. He saw women and children leave the burning MOVE house and enter the rear yard of the house.

Nathan Benner and Thomas Boyd. Police detectives. They knew gasoline was stored on the roof of the MOVE house.

Berghaier, James. Police officer. Risked his life to save Birdie Africa after he fainted face down in a pool of water in the alley.

Biggins, John. Police officer, Bomb Disposal Unit. Refused to testify.

Blackwell, Lucien. Chairman, Finance Committee of City Council. Attended Pre-dawn meeting at Mayor Goode's home on May 13, 1985. The MOVE house was in his council district.

Bond, Clifford. Replaced Mrs. Nichols as block captain. Demanded action by city and state or the neighbors would act.

Boyce, Thomas. Police officer, Bomb Disposal Unit. Refused to testify.

Bronson, Audrey. Member of the investigating commission.

Brooks, Leo. Managing Director of Philadelphia. Retired Army major general who was the city's chief operating officer and who supervised the Osage Avenue operation.

Brown, William. Chairman of the investigating commission. Presided at the public hearings and supervised the commission's deliberations.

Buirrus, Charles. Community activist. Negotiated with MOVE and discussed negotiations with the mayor.

Chinn, Julia. Member of the investigating commission.

Cliett, Eugene. Commissioner, Philadelphia Department of Revenue. Mayor Goode said he told him former Mayor Green had a policy of avoiding conflicts with MOVE.

Coleman, Joseph. President of Philadelphia City Council. Attended pre-dawn meeting at Mayor Goode's home on May 13, 1985. Told the mayor he thought police tactics were excessive.

Connor, Edward. Police Sergeant, Bomb Disposal Unit. He was knocked down by a .38-caliber bullet which struck his bullet-proof vest. He was not injured.

Cooke, M. Tood. Member of the investigating commission.

Craig, John. Police chief inspector. He knew gasoline was stored on the roof of the MOVE house.

Cullen, Edward. Member of the investigating commission.

D'ulisse, Lawrence. Police officer. Stationed at west end of the alley. Saw women and children leave the burning MOVE house and enter the rear yard.

Dibona, G. Fred. Judge. Issued court order which police tried to enforce during the 1978 confrontation with MOVE.

Draper, George. Police officer, Civil Affairs Unit. Forwarded information to his superiors about evidence of a gasoline can on the roof of 6221 Osage Avenue.

Geppart, Richard. President of Geppart Brothers Demolition Co. Offered crane to remove bunker from the roof of the MOVE house.

Goode, W. Wilson. Mayor of Philadelphia. Authorized plan to arrest four MOVE members living at 6221 Osage Avenue on May 13, 1985.

Griffiths, Donald. Police Sergeant, commander of Post Four, overlooking the alley. Detective Stephenson's notes indicated that Griffiths said he shot one of the MOVE men. Griffiths denied shooting anyone and making the statement.

Haskins, Yvonne. Regional Supervisor, Pennsylvania Parole Board. Notified Philadelphia police of parole violation arrest warrant for Frank James Africa. Sought police assistance to arrest him. Police asked her to delay the arrest.

Henderson, Iris. Ward committee person. Met with Osage residents. Contacted city officials about the problems with MOVE.

James, Louise. Owner of 6221 Osage Avenue Former MOVE member. John Africa's sister and Frank James Africa's mother.

Kauffman, Bruce. Member of the investigating commission.

Kelly, James McGirr. Federal District Court judge. Issued order protecting police witnesses from pleading the Fifth Amendment in public.

Kirk, Herbert. Police sergeant. Developed the original police tactical plan.

Klein, William. Police officer, Bomb Disposal Unit. Made the bomb which was dropped on the MOVE house.

Laarkamp, James. Police officer, Bomb Disposal Unit. Refused to testify.

Lillie, Charisse. Member of the investigating commission.

Lytton, William. Staff director and general counsel to the commission.

Mapp, Betty. Resident of the 6200 block of Osage Avenue. Testified at public hearings about problems created by MOVE and the failure of the city to act.

Marandola, Dominick. Police lieutenant. Stationed in alley; overheard saying he saw MOVE members lying in the alley.

Marion, David. Chancellor Philadelphia Bar Association. Wrote letter to commission asking for inquiry into civil rights violations by the city.

Marrazzo, William. Commissioner, Philadelphia Water Department. Mayor Goode said Marrazzo told him former Mayor Green had a policy of avoiding conflict with MOVE.

Marshall, Wayne Butch. MOVE'S neighbor on Osage Avenue. Fought with MOVE members.

McLaughlin, Edward. Police captain, Major Investigation Division. He knew from photographs that gasoline was stored on the roof of the MOVE house.

Mellor, Charles. Police officer. Stationed in alley when MOVE women and children tried to escape the fire.

Moran, Emerson. Communications officer to the commission.

MOVE. A religious cult. Used the house at 6221 Osage Avenue as a base for psychological warfare against their neighbors to try to force the release of imprisoned members.

Mozenter, Robert. Chief counsel, Fraternal Order of Police.

Mulvihill, Clarence. Police officer. Stationed at west end of the alley.

Murray, Joseph. Fireman. Heard automatic weapons fired in alley when women and children were trying to escape the fire.

Nichols, Howard. Resident of the 6200 block of Osage Avenue Sought police action against MOVE house. Rejected pleas to withdraw complaints against the MOVE house before the police action began.

Nichols, Inez. Block captain of the 6200 Block of Osage Avenue Held meetings of Osage residents.

Nix, Robert N.C. Chief Justice, Pennsylvania Supreme Court. He was mentioned by another judge who offered to intervene and negotiate a review of the trial which MOVE was protesting. He was never contacted.

O'Connor, Maryia. Secretary to the commission.

Pernsley, Irene. Commissioner, Philadelphia Department of Human Services. Received request for information about legal authority to pick up the children. She asked if they were "MOVE children." Did not ask if they were in danger.

Powell, Frank. Police lieutenant, Bomb Disposal Unit. Dropped bomb from helicopter. Refused to testify.

Ramp, James. Police officer. Killed during 1978 confrontation between police and MOVE.

Rementer, Steve. Police officer. Stationed in alley when women and children tried to escape the fire.

Revel, Albert. Police sergeant. He helped to develop the police tactical plan. Knew gasoline was stored on the roof of the MOVE house.

Richmond, William. Philaldelphia Fire Commissioner. Commanded firefighters during confrontation. Agreed with the police commissioner to let the bunker burn.

Rizzo, Frank. Mayor of Philadelphia, 1972 to 1980. He was mayor during the 1978 confrontation between police and MOVE.

Ruth, Henry S. Jr. Member of the investigating commission.

Sambor, Gregore. Philadelphia Police Commissioner. Led police assault on the MOVE house. Agreed with the fire commissioner to let the bunker burn.

Scipione, Frank J. Philadelphia Deputy Fire Commissioner. Police told him not to turn water on the fire.

Shanahan, James. Police captain. He knew gasoline was stored on the roof of the MOVE house.

Shanahan, Neil. Chief investigator to the commission.

Sims, LaVern. John Africa's sister. Testified at public hearings.

Singley, Carl. Special Counsel to the commission.

Skarbeck, John. Battalion chief, Philadelphia Fire Department. Heard a police sergeant say he shot one of the MOVE men.

Stephenson, William. Police detective. Assigned to make contemporaneous notes during the confrontation. His notes provided valuable information.

Stewart, William (PUMPKIN). Police officer, weapons specialist. Assigned to Post Four, overlooking the alley. Gave a statement that he heard police gunfire in the alley but testified that he did not hear police gunfire.

Sutton, Gloria. Case worker, Philadelphia Commission on Human Relations. Organized meetings of Osage Avenue residents.

Swans, Bennie. Executive Director, Crisis Intervention Network. He and his assistants worked to restrain the spectators who became violently angry when no one fought the fire.

Tate, James H. J. Mayor, of Philadelphia, 1963 to 1971.

Tate, Raymond. Deputy Commissioner, Philadelphia Department of Licenses and Inspections. Testified that when he served as commissioner of the department it was his policy to avoid enforcing the law at the MOVE house.

Teti, Ralph. Deputy City Solicitor, City of Philadelphia.

Tiers, John. Police inspector. He knew gasoline was stored on the roof of the MOVE house.

Tolbert, Paul. Police officer. Stationed in the alley when women and children tried to escape the fire.

Trudel, William. Police officer. Assigned to Post Four, overlooking the alley. He saw women and children leave the burning house and enter the rear yard of the MOVE house.

Truman, Peter. Pennsylvania state legislator Philadelphia and ward leader. Ayyended pre-dawn meeting at Mayor Goode's home on May 13, 1985. The MOVE house was in his district. The mayor assured him the children would be protected.

Tursi, Michael. Police officer. Helped to develop the police tactical plan. Knew gasoline was stored on the roof of the MOVE house. Stationed in rear alley when children tried to escape the fire.

Vaccarelli, John. Lieutenant, Philadelphia Fire Department. Heard automatic weapons fired in the alley when women and children tried to escape the fire.

Washington, Paul. Member of the investigating commission.

Welch, Neil J. Member of the investigating commission.

Williams, Hardy. Pennsylvania State Senator. Personal friend and political ally of Mayor Goode. The MOVE house was in his district. Told the mayor to stop the assault on the MOVE house.

Williams, Novella. Community leader. Negotiated with MOVE members and neighbors. Talked to the mayor on May 13, 1985 and asked him to withdraw police. Warned him someone would be killed.

Williams, Robert. Judge, Commonwealth Court of Pennsylvania. Told Gerald Africa he was willing to contact Chief Justice Nix to obtain a review of the trial of imprisoned MOVE members.

Wilson, Lloyd and Lucretia. Neighbors who lived next door to the MOVE house. Driven out of their home by MOVE.

Wolfinger, Robert. Chief Inspector, Philadelphia Police Department. Asked Mrs. Haskins to delay arrest warrant for Frank Africa.